Best wishes
Ronnie

QUOTE

"No man is a failure who has friends." (From

"It's not the hand you're dealt in life that

(Tony Garnett, producer of Kes at the unveiling of the Blue Plaque in honour

of Barry Hines in 2019)

"I thoroughly enjoyed reading Ronnie Steele's tales of growing up in Barnsley. They are funny, sad, and vividly authentic."

Richard Hines
(Author of No Way But Gentlenesse. A Memoir of how Kes, my kestrel, changed my life).

DEDICATION

I'm dedicating this book to all the children I taught during my twenty-eight years as a primary school teacher in my home town of Barnsley. It might sound clichéd but it's nevertheless true, that they taught me far more than I taught them.

ACKNOWLEDGEMENTS

Heartfelt thanks to my partner, Janet Richardson, for her support, patience and advice while editing my work. Also, many thanks to Richard Hines for his encouragement and for re-editing many of the stories.

The following people deserve much credit for providing information, without which, none of these stories could have been written:

Ged Wilcock, Garry Blake, Melv Henighan, Dave Riddiough, Steve Robson, Paul Wilkinson, Stan Mincher, Rob Rookledge, Michael Bray, Ian Bailey, Charles Salter, Rob Sherriff, Chris Rawlinson and to many others who have contributed to this book without even being aware of it.

Ronnie Steele. September 2021.

Chapter Headings:

1. RONNIE STEELE (1923 – 1944) – My namesake
2. MY DAD IS MY HERO - Part One
3. THE CREAM ALWAYS RISES TO THE TOP – Rob Rookledge: The ordinary lad with the extraordinary story
4. THE PETER WEBSTER SHOW – When the whole of Barnsley migrates to Blackpool
5. THE TRAGIC DEATH OF CHRISTOPHER ENOCH (1954 to 1964)
6. HAROLD RUSHFORTH - The head teacher who makes a difference
7. THE REAL BRIAN GLOVER - Summer 1966
8. BORN LUCKY
9. OUR VERY FIRST LESSON WITH MR HINES - September 1966
10. BARRY HINES AND HIS HILARIOUS ONE-LINERS - Spring 1967
11. MR HINES FACES A CLASS REVOLT - February 1967
12. BRIAN GLOVER SAVES MY LIFE - April 1967
13. THE WINDS OF CHANGE AVOID LONGCAR CENTRAL
14. THE SHEER BRILLIANCE OF MR GLOVER - April 1968
15. BARRY HINES AND THE PUDDING BALL - Summer 1968
16. THE PEAKS AND TROUGHS OF PLAYING FOR BARNSLEY BOYS – 1968/9
17. MY VERY BRIEF CAREER AS A COAL MINER
18. OUT OF THE MOUTHS OF BABES - 1985
19. IAN BAILEY BUMPS INTO BRIAN GLOVER - 1990
20. MEETING BARRY HINES AGAIN AND SOME SIGNIFICANT SUBSEQUENT EVENTS - 1994
21. MY DAD IS MY HERO - Part Two
22. MY DAD IS MY HERO – The squeakiest wheel gets most oil
23. LOOK WHAT THEY'VE DONE TO MY SONG, MA – Murdering creativity
24. BARRY HINES'S FUNERAL - March 2016
25. THE TOPSY-TURVY WORLD OF STATUE-BUILDING
26. BUILD IT AND THEY WILL COME

First published in the United Kingdom by Arc Publishing and Print 2021
Copyright © Ronnie Steele 2021

All rights reserved. No portion of this book may be reproduced, stored in a retrieval system or transmitted at any time or by any means mechanical, electronic, photocopying, recording or otherwise, without the prior written permission of the publisher.

The right of Ronnie Steele to be identified as the author of this work has been asserted by him in accordance with the Copyright, Designs and Patents Act 1988.

The information in this book is given in good faith and is believed to be correct at the time of publication.
Neither the author or the publisher accepts any responsibility for errors or omissions.
All views and comments in this book are those of the author and should not be attributed to the publisher.

WHO'S RONNIE STEELE AND WHY HAS HE WRITTEN THIS BOOK?

Ronnie Steele grew up on the Athersley South Council Estate, Barnsley, but his family moved into the town centre in 1960. He attended Racecommon Road Infants then Agnes Road Juniors. He spent three years of his secondary education at Longcar Central, where he was taught by Barry Hines and Brian Glover.

In 1968 he moved to Holgate Grammar School where he was selected to play for the successful Barnsley Boys' football team.

In 1970, Ronnie signed as an apprentice professional footballer for his beloved Barnsley, and despite a series of injuries, showed great promise and made plenty of appearances for the reserves. Unfortunately, he played his last game at Oakwell against Halifax Town Reserves in April 1972 when he limped off with a knee injury. At the time he was still only seventeen years old. Five months later, an operation revealed Ronnie was suffering from "early changes of osteoarthritis" and was given the devastating news by the surgeon he would never be able to play professional football again.

In 1974, Ronnie began a career in the civil service but after six months he hated it so much he chose to leave. Instead, he proposed to use some of his compensation from the English Football Association, to finance his way through teacher-training college in Retford. He then enjoyed many years teaching in several Barnsley primary schools.

In 1997 his career in Education came full circle when he took up a teaching post at Richard Newman Primary School. This was the school that Ronnie first attended as a child, and he was then given the very same classroom he was once taught in – Room One.

In 2016 he decided to try and pay tribute to his favourite school teacher, Barry Hines, by raising money to build a statue in his honour, in Barnsley town centre. With the help of six friends, the Kes Group raised the necessary funds and the finished statue was unveiled by Ken Loach and David Bradley in November 2021.

In 2019, the former deputy head teacher, author and film-maker, Richard Hines (brother of the late Barry) took the Kes Group on a tour of the Hoyland sites used in filming the iconic movie, Kes. With the blessing of Richard Hines, Ronnie himself now conducts four tours a year.

By writing this book, Ronnie aims not only to draw the world's attention to the extraordinary lives of ordinary people, but to also make sure these important social histories are never forgotten.

Ronnie is divorced and has two grown-up children. Since retiring from teaching, he's spent much of his spare time singing semi professionally in local pubs and clubs, and writing prose and poetry. He's also well known as a keen trade unionist, political activist and public speaker.

Mam and Dad at Military Cemetery Bari.

CHAPTER ONE

RONNIE STEELE (1923 TO 1944) – My namesake

My dad is born at 30 Harvey Street, the youngest of five children, on Armistice Day 1927. His older brother, Ronnie, is his best friend and hero. There's four years between them and they get up to all the usual boyhood pranks, but by and large they have a happy and loving childhood. There must be some trauma in the family when their two year-old sister, Peggy, dies but somehow they manage to cope with this. Ronnie himself does fine at school, passing his 11 Plus at Agnes Road and being selected for a place at Mark Street Central School. In 1941, at the age of 18, after spending nearly four years working at Carlton Brickyard, Ronnie is 'called-up' to fight the fascists in World War II. He sees action in North Africa where he's wounded in the shoulder. On his return to England to convalesce he has the opportunity to be invalided out of the army but instead he chooses to rejoin his comrades-in-arms in the Mediterranean region. Sadly, in 1944, Ronnie is mortally wounded fighting in Southern Italy and though he survives for five weeks, he eventually dies. This tragedy obviously has a devastating effect on my dad and all the Steele family.

However, life goes on and in 1949 my dad marries Mary Bray, originally from Union Street on the infamous Barnsley Barebones. Soon my sister and I are born to complete our little branch of the Steele clan. My parents decide to name me after Uncle Ron and as soon as we're old enough to understand, Dad tells us stories about his brother when he was young. For instance, every Xmas we hear the tale about when they went carol-singing to Mrs O'Brien's on Harvey Street. Ronnie is so desperate to take a leak he disappears round the corner and leaves my dad to 'hold the fort'. However, half way through the song my dad forgets the words to "*In the Bleak Mid Winter*" so he stops singing and follows his brother round the corner saying,

"Ron! Ron! I've forgotten the words. What comes next?"

It did seem funny when we heard it first time but after that it's only my dad that laughs at the tale. We're far too respectful though to remind him that we've already heard it a million times.

Every so often throughout our childhood, Dad brings a big box down from the loft that contains photos and memorabilia relating to Uncle Ron. I spend ages trying on his Desert Rat's cap and the elasticated, tinted goggles that he wore for protection from the harsh desert sun and I often play with the many medals he was awarded. I read over and over again, his letters from North Africa, and the correspondence to my Grandma and Granddad Steele from the matron who nursed Ronnie until his death. There's also a poignant letter sent to the family from his best friend and military oppo, Ron White of Wath.

One day my dad relates a story to us about his brother that obviously troubles him. This is how he sets the scene:

It's 1943 and Ronnie has fully recovered from a shoulder wound and is given the choice to return to North Africa or get a job in Blighty.

"Why do you want to go back to fight, Ron?" asks my dad, as his brother polishes-up his army boots before setting off to the railway station.

"To be honest I'm not sure, Fred. I've trained and lived and fought with my comrades and it just feels, I don't know, kind-alike natural to return to them and fight alongside them once more. So I want to go back, Fred. I MUST go back. Something deep inside is forcing me back and I think it's beyond my control.

Fred proudly picks up his brother's heavy kitbag and walks beside him, heading down Racecommon Road and up Shambles Street to the old Courthouse Railway Station in the centre of town. It's Thursday 5th August 1943 and when they set off walking, the sun is just setting on the western horizon. By 8:30 pm the sky is dark and they're sat on a bench waiting for the train. It's too humid to sit in the waiting room. The station is quiet except for a couple of soldiers, a railway worker and the ticking of two enormous clocks. As they sit waiting, Fred has this terrible premonition. He tries to push it away but the harder he tries, the more it returns to his consciousness. Then the feeling becomes a thought and soon a nagging voice in his head says... This is the last time you're ever going to see, Ron. The very last time you're ever going to see him.

As the train squeals to a halt at the platform and releases its steam, Fred manages to tell Ron what's bothering him:

"You've got to make sure you survive this, Ron. Tell me you'll survive. Tell me that we'll see each other again. Tell me! Please!"

"What? Yeah, of course we will, you daft ha'porth" says Ron, picking up his rifle and kitbag. "Of course we'll see each other again. Don't you be fretting about me. You just make sure you look after Mam and Dad." Ronnie then boards the train and pushes down the window as the steam engine slowly pulls away at the behest of the guard's red flag and whistle.

When Dad finishes telling us this story and we're back in the present, he simply adds, "I'll see my brother, one day. I know I will."

Almost 40 years after Ron's death, Mam and Dad are dropped off from the mini bus on the outskirts of the coastal City of Bari, Southeast Italy. It's May 1983 and the morning temperature is just about bearable. The sign on the attractive stone-built enclosure reads:

BRITISH AND COMMONWEALTH MILITARY CEMETERY

Dad has imagined this place for the last 40 years and it's even more beautiful and peaceful than he ever envisaged. It's all rolling hills and neatly patterned olive groves. There's no sounds of the city in this rural corner of Puglia- only the music of nature. Now they have to locate Ron's headstone.

A man in his 50s with a moustache, emerges from a tiny cottage built in the corner of the cemetery. Behind him is a black-haired woman with olive skin.

"Buongiorno! Buongiorno!" Shouts a man. "Mr and Missus Steele. We been expecting you. I, Carlo and this my wife, Livia. We... um... responsible for tending graves here including Ronald's" he says as he extends his arm to shake hands. "We first show you where is grave and then we leave you in peace for contemplazione" and then Carlo and his wife head towards the grave. When they're about thirty metres away, Carlo points to the row where it can be found and then he and Livia go no further.

As soon as my dad sees the grave, he's overwhelmed. It's just far too much for him to cope with. He's waited for this moment ever since that hot evening at the Courthouse Station in August 1943.

Suddenly, dad begins to shed the things he's carrying. First his shoulder bag falls on the grass and as he walks faster, his camera drops to the floor. Then he breaks into a trot and the bouquet of flowers spill onto the path... and my dad's shouting at the top of his voice,

'Ron! Ron! I'm here Ron! I'm here! I swore I'd see you again. I swore it, Ron! And I'm here just like I promised!'. Then he falls to his knees on the grave and howls inconsolably... while forty years of pent-up grief flows from his heart and runs down his cheeks. It's so painful for my mam to witness. All she can do is embrace and comfort him.

Later, when the flowers had been neatly arranged on the grave and emotions have settled down a bit, Carlo and Livia, the cemetery sextons, approach them with a tray of refreshments. They too feel very emotional. For many years they have tended these graves and are keen to hear the back-story of those they have grown to love.

Mam and dad then sign the visitors' attendance book, which is in a bronze cupboard at the graveyard entrance.

After an hour the mini-bus returns and it's time for them to leave. All four of them hug and kiss like they are very close brothers and sisters.

My mother dies in 1990 but dad is still alive and kicking in 2015 when my partner, Janet, and I get the opportunity ourselves to make the 1500 mile pilgrimage from Barnsley to Bari. When we arrive, we see the sexton's cottage has disappeared,

otherwise the place is unchanged from the old photographs. Our visit is the fulfilment of a life-time's ambition for me, and my heart is satisfied that I've seen for myself, that corner of a foreign field that is forever England.

War is such a terrible thing.

Uncle Ron

CHAPTER TWO

MY DAD IS MY HERO: Part One

My Dad opens his eyes after forty winks in the armchair. It's early Wednesday evening in late August 1958 and he's been on the day-shift at the nearby New Carlton Colliery. Fred is below average height and slightly built but this belies his wiry strength as a coal-face worker. At school he'd been a true working-class scholar but as was often the case in war time, financial necessity demanded he start work on the day he left Holgate Grammar School. Today's been such a hot day that Dad has most of the windows open. The heat has even caused the tar in the road to melt. He rubs his eyes and stands to look out of the front window and feels a slight welcoming draught. Fred looks in the mirror above the fireplace and smoothes down his thinning hair with his right palm. Except for the ticking clock on the mantelpiece, number 73 Highfield Avenue is very quiet because Mary, my mum, is visiting her parents on Thrumpton Road, on the neighbouring estate, with me and my sister in tow. Danny Oates' ice cream van starts playing its familiar jingle just outside the Stokes's house on the opposite side of street. It was probably his chimes that woke Dad in the first place. He decides to make a pot of tea and through the back window he sees the rear garden with the kiddies swing and beyond that a very large sloping field filled with tall, wild grass and blackened patches. It's only three weeks since someone set fire to the field and it took all the men from the street to go out with sacks and spades to overcome it. Then, casting his eyes beyond the field he can just see the Smithies Council Estate where the brilliant Tommy Taylor was raised and Dad's mind focuses on how he was so tragically killed in the Munich Air Disaster only a few weeks before. Dad decides to make sandwiches for work and also for Mam, my sister and myself, for when we return. Then he gets out the iron and attacks the small pile of clothes that need attention. As he smoothes the creases out of a t-shirt, he sings a new song by the Everly Brothers using the words he's written on the back of a cornflake box. He finds he has to write them down because his instruction in French and Latin at Holgate, put him off memorising by rote, for a lifetime. His eyes keep flitting from the lyrics cellotaped to the kitchen door, to the collar and sleeves of the shirt.

"I can make you mine

Taste your lips of wine

Anytime night of day

Only trouble is, gee wizz

I'm dreaming my life away..."

Meanwhile my Mam is tidying the contents of an old sideboard while Grandma makes my sister and me a cold beef sandwich. Grandma always makes the very best sandwiches: homemade bread, best butter from the Coop and beef that's been cut on the bacon slicer at Triggy's General Stores. Granddad is fast asleep in bed as usual at this time. He works regular nights at Monk Bretton Colliery but every afternoon he likes a few pints in the Manx Pub in town. Mam's older brother, Uncle Ernest, has finished his shift at the brewery and is lying on his back, as usual, on the rug, next to the hearth, snoring. He works as a delivery driver's mate. It suits him down to the ground because he's a big strong guy which is useful for shifting heavy beer barrels but he's also known as someone who won't refuse a pint at any pub they deliver to, so he often finishes his shift fairly well-oiled. This wouldn't matter one jot except when he's drunk, Uncle Ernest is one of those people who'd rather have a fight than his dinner.

My Mam tries on a salmon-pink cardigan she's found in the cupboard. "Do you wear this cardie, Mam?" she asks Grandma as she walks into the kitchen.

"Oh no, love. It's a bit small for me. Edith Allott gave me it last year. You know Edith... she married one of the Chadwick's. Oooo, wait a minute. I tell a lie. She didn't marry one of the Chadwick's, she..."

"Aye, alright Mam" says my mother laughing "I don't want its family history. I just need to know if you still wear it."

"No, love, you can..."

"Ey up" shouts Ernest, waking up from his stupor. "Who's making all the bleeding noise?"

"Oh, here we go" says Mam. "Mr Nasty's woke up, has he? Why don't you do what normal people do and nap in bed?"

"I'll knock your bleeding teeth out if you don't shut it" says Ernest scratching his crotch.

"Oi, Ernest!" shouts Grandma. "That's enough! There's bairns here!"

"I'm not bothered who's here. I'll knock their bleeding teeth out an' all."

"Oh aye" says Mam "You're very good at threatening bairns, aren't you? Bet you wouldn't say that if Fred was here." And it was that response from my Mam that was enough to make Uncle Ernest completely flip his lid.

"Oh wouldn't I? We'll soon see how tough little Freddie-Boy is" says Ernest, staggering to his feet and putting on his work-boots. "I'll knock *his* bleeding neck in an' all!" He stuffs a packet of Woodbine and a box of matches into his pocket and is out of the side door, heading for the bus stop by the red telephone box on Ollerton Road, before anyone can stop him.

My Mam flies into a panic because she knows what her brother is capable of. His temper and acts of violence are legendary. She realises she has to forewarn my Dad somehow but no one she knows has a car or a telephone. She shouts her younger brother, Michael, down from his bedroom. He's a thirteen year old student at Edward Sheerien.

"Mike! Mike! Ernest is blathered and he's going to pick a fight with Fred! You've got to get to our house before Ernest and warn him!"

Michael puts his pumps on and runs for the bus but it's already been and gone and is just negotiating the Newstead Road roundabout with Ernest on board, seething. So he sets off running the mile and a half to Highfield Avenue. It's so humid, he has to keep stopping to catch his breath. He passes a Danny Oates ice-cream van as he navigates the side streets of Athersley South Estate. On the pavement is a runny blob of yellow icecream that someone's dropped and it's oozing blood-red strawberry juice, which he has to niftily leap over. By the time he reaches the bottom of Highfield Avenue, Michael's dripping with sweat and his breathing sounds asthmatic. As he crosses the bottom of the street from where the Rookledge family lives, he hears a buzz of activity outside number 73. Oh no! Mike thinks: It's happened. I'm too late! Ernest has got to Fred and done his foul deed.

As he gets nearer the house, still panting like a dog, he sees two burly figures carrying my dad out of the door at the side and down the concrete path, unconscious. But it's not my Dad at all, it's Uncle Ernest's lifeless-looking body that's getting bumped and dumped near the garden gate. Ernest hasn't a scratch on him but his lips are blue and he's in need of emergency medical treatment.

"What's happened?" says Michael.

"Haven't a clue" says the fellow nearest the gate. We heard such a commotion. There was banging and shouting and crashing and then Fred comes out and asks us to help carry this bloke out of his house. He points down at the body. Look at him, he's spark out. Don't know what Fred clobbered him with because he's not left a mark on him.

I'm four years old at the time and the events on Highfield Avenue that day are kept from me and my sister. The row at my Grandma's is also never mentioned again so is largely forgotten. However, forty-two years later, Michael tells me the whole story from thread to needle for the very first time. I go up to ask my Dad, who's now a 73 year old widower, for his version. This is what he tells me:

"I'm sitting in the armchair in the living room at home after making some sandwiches and finishing off the bit of ironing for your Mam when I hear someone come in through the back door. At first I think it's your Mam with you and our Pauline but when I look up it's your Uncle Ernest. He just walks straight over to me and without any warning head-butts me with all his might on the bridge of my nose. It's totally unexpected. I'm in a state of shock. I can't think. After a few seconds I feel a rising anger and a great flush of adrenalin forces me up on my feet and I'm grappling to save my life..." says my Dad." Then my Dad suddenly stops.

"And?" I say.

"And what?" says Dad.

"What happens next?" I say.

"Nothing" he says. "I quickly get the better of Ernest and he soon collapses. That's all there was to it. But always remember this, Ronnie: If you're ever attacked, it's better to fight with your brain than your fists."

"But Dad... what did you actually do to get the better of Uncle Ernest?"

"Oh, it wasn't a big deal. I was just too quick-thinking for him, that's all" says Dad getting up from his chair.

And that is that. Dad turns on the TV news to indicate, to my irritation, that the conversation is over. I do eventually discover all the minute details but it takes me another twelve months and the revelation is accidental. Until then I wonder almost every day how my slightly-built, peace-loving Dad, beat off a surprise attack by a fourteen stone bully and put him to sleep in seconds. No blood, no boasting: like David knocking out Goliath, with one hand tied behind his back.

What a hero!

CHAPTER THREE

THE CREAM ALWAYS RISES TO THE TOP – Rob Rookledge: The ordinary lad with the extraordinary story

Robert Rookledge and I are born at the same time and in the same place. I come into this world on 16th May 1954 and he's born just a few days later; I live at 73 Highfield Avenue, on Athersley South, and he lives just around the corner on Athersley Road. There aren't too many cars around in the 50s so, even as infants, we are safe to play together on the street.

In 1959 we even start Richard Newman Infants together and Miss Eyre is our reception class teacher. We're in Room One, on bottom corridor. Neither of us is impressed by school that day; the inside of classroom smells of wax crayons, and the outside stinks of sulphur from the coal boilers. Just before morning playtime, Miss Eyre goes to great lengths to explain that there's a small bottle of milk for each of us, and how it'll make us big and strong. Rob says he doesn't like milk so he's going to ask for a cup of tea. He passes me his full milk bottle and goes to place his order for weak tea with one sugar please, with the teacher. Apparently, Miss Eyre says he can't choose tea, or coffee and he certainly can't refuse his warm milk, either. What sort of place is this? Then dinner time's spoilt by the smell of boiled cabbage and Sandra Leigh who has an accident in her knickers. Miss Eyre doesn't half scream at her. Rob says he wants to hug Sandra but he's a bit scared of Miss Eyre.

When the bell goes for afternoon playtime, all the kids rush for the exit door, cheering and screaming, thinking it's home-time. Somehow, Rob and I make it out of the building and onto the school drive, and as there's no one to greet us, we think it's only sensible to head for the campus gates on Wingfield Road and then home.

"I don't like that place" I say to Rob. "I don't think I'll be coming back."

"I'm not either" answers Rob, and just as we reach the school gates we bump into our mothers walking together towards school to pick us up. They're both flabbergasted.

"What on earth are you two doing out of school at this time? You're not supposed to finish until half three" says the red-haired, Mrs Rookledge.

"Bet these two little buggers have absconded" says my mam, and even though I've no idea what 'absconded' means, I've a vague notion that it's not a good thing to do. "We better turn for home" says my mam "and sort it out with Miss Eyre, tomorrow."

"Tomorrow!" shouts Rob. "But I don't like school, mum. I think I'll stay at home and have a cup of tea." And I'm thinking... well if Rob Rookledge isn't going back to that horrible place, I'm certainly not. Then our two mothers communicate with each other using only their eyes.

Next day, Rob and I, are forced onto the treadmill. That whole first year at Richard Newman Infants is awful. Admittedly, learning to read is easy enough. They split us into groups and sit us down on the carpet to memorise a list of words on strips of cards, but the books we're then given containing those words are absolute nonsense. Rob once looks at me and says, "Dick and Dora" and pulls a horrible face, and I reply, "Janet and John" and pretend I'm being sick. Rob and I both wonder why on earth anybody would ever volunteer to read a book? Reading's rubbish!

At the end of our first year, my parents buy a house on Harvey Street, in Barnsley, but it's not the end of my friendship with Rob because he often visits his Nanna Wyatt on Havelock Street. That's the next street to us and we're less than a hundred yards apart. Furthermore, Robert tells me his mum has a hole in her heart and when she has a hospital stay, he lives at his nans. That's just perfect for me because he comes to my school, Agnes Road Juniors for Boys, for short periods and it's brilliant there, I love it. Not only that but our teacher, Miss Thorpe, let's Rob sit next to me so I can 'show him the ropes'.

By the time we're nine, Rob and I are closer as mates than we've ever been. We're both mad about football, cricket, athletics and boxing and we're both dorky-handed*. I teach him how to swear and he teaches me some big words to use in my compositions like 'perilous' and 'confronted'. We're both into reading books, magazines and newspapers by now, but only if it's about sport. Rob in particular knows everything there is to know about Tottenham Hotspurs and that's when I first hear about Jimmy Greaves, Dave Mackay, Bill Nicholson and White Hart Lane.

As he sits next to me I notice that although his handwriting is not joined-up and looks immature, his command of the English language is advanced for his years because he's a real bright spark. However, one terrible day, tragedy strikes.

Rob makes his way up the ginnell from Havelock Street, to call for me for school. I hear his usual knock and open the door to let him in. Like all visitors, he stands on the mat next to the chair. Then he starts talking to both me and my dad and they're words that will live with me until the day I die.

"I've got a secret to tell you" he says. "My mum died last night".

"Oh, Robert" says my dad, "I'm so, so sorry to hear that".

And that's it. Although my dad is obviously very upset by the tragic news, Robert seems okay and so am I. We both know that death is serious and upsetting because we've seen how it affects adults close to us but we're both too young to understand the finality of it.

Robert's nanna, uncle and dad make the decision early that Robert comes to live permanently in Havelock Street. His nan becomes his new mum and his brilliant Uncle Arnie becomes his new dad and for the next five years Rob and I are inseparable. We do everything that best mates do: We go 'bunny-wooding'; carol singing; exploring; we compete in athletics meetings at the Dorothy Hyman stadium; we buy the same clothes; we watch Barnsley FC play home and away; we follow every event in the '64 Olympics in Japan; we're both madly in love with Lillian Board, the athlete; we represent Agnes Road at the Shaw Lane Athletics gala and the Barnsley Swimming Gala; we go abroad together with the school; we play football and cricket in our backyard; we even get a job together working part-time at Becket's pop factory during the holidays (quite illegally); when it's raining we play table tennis, monopoly or cards in our front room; we chase after girls at the Civic and The Georges; we fall-out and fall-in; and we fight and make friends again.

"Our Ronnie and Robert, they're just like blood brothers" my mam used to say when gossiping with relatives and neighbours.

When Robert and I fall-out it's usually to do with a dispute over who won what and when... or a row over a game we're both competing in. One really hot summer's day when we're twelve, Robert and I go into Shawland's field to play cricket. There's only the two of us but we can manage. A hard corkie would be preferable but we have to make-do with a small sponge ball. We set up stumps and Robert wins the toss and bats first. He's a skilful left-handed batter but he gets lucky a few times. However, once he's got his eye-in, he starts knocking me all over the field. I occasionally bowl a pearler and anticipate it smashing into the stumps but instead he takes a big swing at it and it finishes flying down the hill with me racing after it. I'm really tired and frustrated in the heat, while he gets more expansive. I appeal for LBW a few times but he'll not be conned by that. Eventually, after scoring 55 runs, I bowl Robert out and I'm now more than ready to exact my revenge. He grabs the spongy and gets ready to bowl at me. After shouting "Play" he takes a short run-up and over comes his left arm. It's an incredibly poor effort. It's just begging to be smashed out of the field. It's not even on target, so I swing my bat as hard as I can but the 'spongy' hits a divot and changes course, beats my bat and knocks down my middle stump. Out first ball for a flaming duck and Rob can't stop laughing. So I chase after him with the bat because I'm a terrible loser; but he's fresh and I'm knackered. After about ten minutes we collapse in a heap, laughing and we are best mates again. Now Rob suggests we play a game of *Mercy*. I can beat him any day at this. *Mercy* is a game where you're tested to see how much pain you can stand before you cry for 'mercy' to end the torture. Then an older mate joins us and Rob invites him to be the torturer. Carl agrees and tries the Chinese Torture on my wrist, first. I think I'm tough but Carl is not even trying that hard, before I'm screaming,

"Mercy! Mercy! Mercy!" and the torture ends.

I'm wondering how much pain Robert can withstand. He's surely not as tough as me, is he? Carl starts off with a gentle twist of Rob's wrist and I soon see a twinge of pain flash across his face. Hmmm, he's hurting already, so it's only a matter of time before he gives in. However, as Carl twists harder, Rob starts to relax and shows he can obviously cope. Then more pressure is exerted by Carl and even his own face starts to go red, but Rob is still unflinching. "Reight" says Carl, as he applies maximum force on poor Robert's wrist. But Robert just closes his eyes and lowers his head. He must be suffering like mad but he'll not give in. Then Carl applies so much pressure that he himself is moaning from the effort, but Rob is silent. I scrutinise Carl's face and he's looking worried. Nobody can stand this amount of force... but Rob Rookledge proves he can. Carl tires, decides he can't continue and so lets go. Rob turns over and puts his head in his arms for a good five minutes in order to recover. Is he crying? Is he heck. This is a game-changer. I realise Rob is made of much sterner stuff than I am.

Sometimes I go with Rob to visit his dad in Athersley. On one particular day, his dad is cutting the grass when Rob tells me he has something secret to show me. He opens the drawer of the sideboard in the dining room and lifts out several envelopes.

"Look what I've found" he says. I cast my eyes across the very official-looking documents to see they are adoption papers. Rob was adopted as a baby and his original name was Thomas Willets. This is almost as big a shock to me as it must have been to Rob.

When I tell my mam and dad about this, they confide that Rob was adopted because his mam couldn't have a baby; her hole-in-the-heart condition meant giving birth was far too risky. Then the penny drops. Is this the reason why my parents have such a special affinity for Rob? Could it be why they always take Robert's side when I fall-out with him?

Robert goes to Holgate Grammar and I go to Longcar Central but we still see each other every day. Once when my mam's in town shopping, Robert comes to mine and we discuss the bad luck that our mate, Roy Ward, has had by breaking his leg playing football.

"I hope I never break my leg, touch wood" says Robert, and he taps the wooden arm of the chair he's sat in.

Exactly a fortnight later, my mam and dad tell me to sit down because they've something important to tell me. I can tell it's something very serious by the grave look on both their faces.

"If it's about nicking those apples..." I start to say but my dad stops me half way through the sentence to say,

"No, Ronnie. It's far more serious than that. It's about Robert. He's been knocked down by a car" And I see my mam put her head in her hands.

"Oh, no! Oh, no! Please, please, don't tell me he's dead. Please!" I say and my sobbing prevents me saying anything else that's coherent.

"No, no, no" says my dad quickly. He's not dead but he is very poorly. He's got some head injuries and his leg is badly smashed up. The surgeons say he'll survive but it'll take a long, long time for him to recover.

That evening I go with his dad to see visit Robert in Becketts Hospital. He's such a terrible sight, I feel sick and dizzy and pass out. The nurse says it was caused by the shock. Robert is still heavily medicated and mumbles something about 'attention-seeking'. He's still funny, is Robert, even when he's drugged-up.

Rob has to spend months in Becketts and has countless operations on his lower leg bones. Fortunately, he soon recovers from his head injuries. While he's healing, the slums of Havelock Street, Longcar Street and Shaw Street are demolished and his Nanna Wyatt and Uncle Arnie are re-housed in a beautiful council semi just off Broadway. So when Robert is finally well enough to return home, it's a completely different environment he returns to.

With that physical distance between us, and Rob not being as active as he once was, we very slowly drift apart as best mates. By the time we leave school, Robert's got a whole new group of friends and so have I, therefore we rarely bump into each other. However, I definitely consider him my blood brother, and always will.

Robert Rookledge is a person who suffers the cruellest of misfortune but never once do I witness him displaying a smidgen of self-pity. But why should he? He's a gifted lad with more love surrounding him than most folk dream of.

After leaving school, Robert accepts an apprenticeship in engineering and is so successful, he eventually becomes the boss of fifty engineers at one of the most advanced coal mines in the world. He marries a lovely Barnsley lass and they create a beautiful family together.

* Local slang for left-handed.

Rob Rookledge with his wife, Di and son Alex

CHAPTER FOUR

THE PETER WEBSTER SHOW – When the whole of Barnsley migrates to Blackpool

It's 1963, I'm nine years old, and we're half-way through our fantastic family holiday in Blackpool. To some, Blackpool is so common, they vow they wouldn't be seen dead there. To others, especially the stars of the small screen, appearing at Blackpool is the very pinnacle of their career; and to those millions of ordinary folk who seek a week away from the daily grind, it is *the* place to be. The great thing about Blackpool is, the sun always shines, or so it seems. Anyway, even if it rains, there are so many indoor places to visit, you can be entertained every morning, afternoon and evening for a fortnight, if need be.

My dad works at Dodworth/Redbrook Colliery and he has a quid a week saved out of his wage so we can spend a glorious week in Paradise. There are five of us in our family party: my mam, dad, older sister Pauline, and my Grandma whom we call, Nannan Steele.

It's Barnsley Feast Week when most workplaces close down and it seems almost everybody from the 'tarn' migrates to the Golden Mile on the Fylde Coast. When you're walking on the promenade it's just like walking through Barnsley Market – every few yards you're bumping into someone you know, wearing Kiss-Me-Quick hats or piling onto a horse-drawn carriage heading for the Tower. Blackpool is full to capacity; it's noisy; it's exciting; and it's great fun.

All five of us are sat waiting expectantly for the greatest live comedy show on earth to begin. At least it is to me. We've been coming to Peter Webster's Talent Show, on the Central Pier, every year for as long as I can remember. The gags are the same every year but they never cease to make us laugh out loud. Today, the open-air theatre is packed with pleasure-seekers from Barnsley and Glasgow as our holiday weeks coincide this year.

On the stage in front of us is a musician dressed in evening suit playing on a white grand piano, and at the back are scores of eye-watering prizes to excite young kids.

Peter Webster walks onto the stage to a massive cheer and applause. Unfortunately, the microphone cable gets wrapped around his legs and the harder he tries, the more the thick black wire, binds his feet and ankles. At first he has to hop into the middle of the stage, as though his trousers are round his ankles, then he falls down as the pianist bashes out a loud discordant note.

The audience find this hilarious. Eventually, Peter untangles himself and climbs to his feet. He's in his late 40s and has brushed-back greying hair and a moustache. He never smiles but he often pulls a funny face as though he's just smelled a dead rat.

He tells a few topical gags about Barnsley people and then he silences the Scots with some equally funny put-downs. After warming up the audience Peter sits down on a white chair and sings, Magic Moments, and you realise he's got a brilliant singing voice. He even whistles a verse and I think, wow! How does he do that? It sounds like he has some kind of gadget to help him. It really is clever. However, as he's performing, this guy from off-stage, wearing flat cap and warehouse coat and smoking a Woodbine, keeps coming on stage and walking in front of him and plonking a couple more white chairs either side of him. It's as though the warehouse man doesn't realise a live show is going on. Peter's expression gets more and more irritated because he has to keep leaning to one side to see his audience.

There's huge applause as Peter finishes his song and then he calls up the infant volunteers to play musical chairs. He counts the chairs aloud and finds there are twelve.

"Hmmm", he says, as he counts the kiddies who are lined up on stage facing the audience. When he gets to number 13 there's one little kid left over; one too many. "You can't play" says Peter to the extra kid at the end "so go on, off you go, skedaddle." The kid looks crestfallen and all the audience in unison go "Aw..." as he walks towards the exit steps, his shoulders sagging. But by putting his fingers in his mouth, Peter issues a loud whistle and the little lad stops and turns. Peter motions him back and presents him with a large box containing a bow and arrow and everyone cheers. As the lad walks off again, Peter whistles him back a second time but now he's offering a bright red football. On the third and final whistle the young 'un receives a tall walking stick of Blackpool rock. By now the boy is smiling broadly and the audience is in hysterics.

An enormous doll's tea party set is presented to the little girl who wins the Musical Chairs game, similar to the one my sister got for her main Christmas present, a few years back. These prizes are really sought-after. Then the stage is cleared as we come to the highlight of the afternoon matinee: the talent contest. This is what I've been waiting for since Whitsuntide. I'm too old now for Musical Chairs, so over the school holiday in May, I stay at my Grandma Bray's on Athersley North and learn a catchy little ballad called *Tell Laura I love Her* by Ricky Valance. It's one of my Uncle Mike's favourites, which he sings so beautifully and he teaches me all the lyrics.

When Peter Webster asks for ten volunteers, there's a race for the stage. However, only nine girls and boys climb up the steps but then I notice Peter calls a lad called Jimmy to join us. I'm third up to sing. All the contestants have to sit at the back of the stage with all the wonderful prizes beside us. I don't listen to the first two acts because I'm going through my song lyrics over and over again. It's murder getting half way through a song and then stopping because you can't remember the words. Soon it's my turn. When he announces me as Ronnie Steele from Barnsley, Peter's voice is drowned out by a small aircraft flying directly above the open-air theatre. Everyone looks up to see a bi-plane rumbling along, pulling a banner behind it which reads:

TOWER CIRCUS EVERY EVENING

7:30 START

Peter explains the rumbling noise by rubbing his stomach and saying, "I must stop eating those mushy peas for lunch."

I'm facing the audience with the microphone-stand adjusted to the perfect height. There's no piano accompaniment to start with. The pianist just picks up the key as I start singing and then plays along. I'm very careful not to start singing on too high a note, otherwise I'll never reach the top ones when I come to them. I'm worrying unnecessarily though. My only error throughout my performance is that I forget the lyrics to one of the verses, so I just sing the same verse twice and no one seems to notice. But it's so thrilling when I hear everyone in the audience singing along to the chorus then cheering and clapping.

The next entertainer up is a chubby little girl with short hair, called Victoria from Bury. As soon as the first words come out of her mouth, the audience twig that she has talent. She sings, *On the Good Ship Lollipop* - the Shirley Temple classic. It sounds absolutely terrific but half-way through she gets mixed up with the words and walks off stage, terribly upset. Peter Webster says,

"That girl has the best singing voice I've heard all summer. I think she'll grow up to be a star and it wouldn't surprise me one bit if the next time she appears on the Central Pier, she's topping the bill, with her name on the side of every tram in Blackpool." The audience give a rousing cheer for the poor little girl.

Then there's a young ventriloquist who can talk whilst drinking a glass of water, followed by a genuine Scottish star in the making. It's Jimmy from Glasgow, who was last to be called onto the stage. He's a nine year old comic and singer. Jimmy's so smooth you'd swear he was a professional. His cocky and accomplished routine makes me so envious. Jimmy is the nearest thing to the Clitheroe Kid, I've ever seen. After him, there are two female tap-dancers who've obviously spent many hours honing their skills in the dance-studio and a Spanish guitarist from North Wales who perhaps needs a little more practice time. Finally, it's Reginald's turn from Stalybridge. Reginald is singing the Roy Orbison song: Crying. He sets off and it's clear he's having trouble even with the easy notes and as he reaches the more difficult ones I look at the faces of the audience and they're all screwed up as though they're under torture in a Japanese prisoner-of-war camp. Sadly, Reginald sounds as bad as a dentist's drill so Peter Webster also contorts his face into a pained expression, then walks to the back of the stage and picks up a piece of rope. After a few seconds he turns it into a noose and he creeps up behind the singer just as his voice becomes intolerable. At this stage there's a much greater noise from the audience than from the singer. Hearing the little lad's voice then seeing the look on Peter's face as he holds up the noose, is just too much for some and many in the audience are shedding tears of laughter! As Reginald's voice screeches to a climax, on the very highest note of the song, the whole audience is screaming and cheering and Reginald takes a long bow, convinced he's done superbly well.

It's now time for the audience to make a judgement. There's only nine kids still standing because Victoria has joined her parents back in the audience. There can only be one winner and it must be Scottish Jimmy because he's a class act. Peter

Webster lines us all up at the front of the stage looking towards the audience. He stands behind each singer, one at a time, and as he points at us the audience raise their hands - that's if they think we're any good. Those who don't score highly are given a generous prize and then guided away to the steps. I've a good idea when I'm being judged because I look at my family and all of them have *both* their hands up, including my nannan. I think my nannan would have put her legs in the air if she could have managed it. More than half the audience is from Barnsley and they're all pointing to the sky. At the end there's only two standing: me and Scottish Jimmy.

It's at this stage that Peter Webster announces that Scottish Jimmy also appeared and won at yesterday's matinee and only agreed to come and entertain today to make up the numbers. Therefore, he concludes:

"And so ladies, gentlemen and mantelpieces, I wish to announce that the winner of today's Peter Webster's Talent Show is this young gentleman from glorious Barnsley" and he grabs hold of my wrist and raises it like they did with Cassius Clay when he beat Sonny Liston."

"And so what a terrific set of prizes he's earned. In this box is a gold Sekonda watch with a matching gold-bracelet strap; on top of that there's a brand new crisp ten-bob note; and last but not least here's a beautiful autograph book."

As the appreciative crowd whistle and cheer, Peter has to shout, "That's the end of the show folks. Hope you've enjoyed it. I must tell you, you have been the very best audience we've had in this theatre since... um... yesterday. Now once again here's the young fellow from Barnsley to sing you out. Good bye and God bless!"

"Laura and Tommy were lovers

He wanted to give her everything..."

All my family are as pleased as punch as we walk off the Central Pier and make our way to the crowded beach. Dad hires three deck chairs and we spend the rest of the afternoon basking in the Blackpool sun. He also buys us all an ice-cream and me and my sister spend half an hour at the Punch and Judy Show. Afterwards, we paddle in the sea and sunbathe on towels that my mam brought. Da Doo Ron Ron by the Crystals is being constantly played in the nearby arcades and drifts over to the beach area. My sister tells me she voted with both her hands so she probably won it for me and she reminds me that the Barnsley people in the audience might only have voted for me because I was from Barnsley.

"It's a bit of a fix, really" she says and she's probably right but that doesn't bother me one tiny bit. I'm giving my dad the watch; I'm planning to get Alan Ball's autograph and I've got a brand new ten-bob note which will pay for me to watch Barnsley FC, ten times this season. Yes! "I was only teasing" my sister adds, "I'm very proud of you, really."

My dad reminds us that we're going on a tram to the Pleasure Beach after tea, where there's the Big Dipper, the Grand National, the Dodgems, the Ghost Train, the Wild Mouse, candy floss and fresh doughnuts to look forward to.

"And don't forget tomorrow night" he says. "We're off to the cinema to see Cliff Richard in Summer Holiday."

Now I know what is meant by, "Our cup runneth over".

Blackpool's detractors can ridicule it all they like. The Lancashire resort, to me, is the perfect Paradise.

I often wonder whether Scottish Jimmy grew up to become a household name and whether the shy lass called Victoria from Bury overcame her stage-fright to fulfil her potential.

When my dad dies in December 2015 I sift through his private, treasured belongings and I find the gold watch I won for him 52 years before.

Mam and Dad on there way to Peter Webster's Talent Show in Blackpool

CHAPTER FIVE

THE TRAGIC DEATH OF CHRISTOPHER ENOCH 1954 – 1964

I often wonder how life would have turned out had we decided to do our usual thing that warm Saturday morning in June 1964.

I very rarely consider all the details and have never ever fully discussed this dreadful event with any other human being... and as a result some facts are lost in the mists of time but others are as sharp as if they happened yesterday. So for example, I can't even remember everyone who was involved in our outing that day. I only recall there was me, Harry, Pete, Chris Enoch himself and three others. This is my story of the events of that day and I hope you understand why it's taken 56 years for me to tell it.

It's a warm Friday afternoon in the classroom and a few of my school mates ask me what we could do tomorrow morning. Normally we'd be going to the children's morning matinee at the ABC Cinema but this June weekend a few of us are ready for a change.

"What about the baths?" someone says.

"Yeah, let's go swimming", I say.

So that's it, without any of us realising it, the fateful decision that would change the lives of many people for ever, is made.

It's Saturday morning and I'm walking up the steps between the tall Roman columns at the front of Race Street Public Baths, Barnsley. We pay at the turnstile and as I click-click through into the foyer I see my favourite drinks machine in front of me and a small collection of grey wire baskets to the side. I pick up a basket to take into the pool area. It's to put my clothes in. On opening the door to the swimming pool I find the scene to be utterly crazy. I don't much notice the powerful odour of the chlorine, instead I'm overcome by the cacophony of reverberating noise: shouting, screaming, splashing, running, diving, jumping, bombing, swimming, ducking, laughing.

It's a madhouse.

We all quickly change and hand in our untidy baskets of over-flowing clothes for safe-keeping then it's straight into any tiny space we can find in the pool. Like a basketful of caught fish we thrash around with no prospect of swimming anywhere. It's no fun at all. I lose my mates. As I stand in the shallow end I get pushed and shoved, banged and splashed.

I bump into Harry.

"Ey up, Ronnie. Pete wants to know if we should go into the deep end?"

"Aye. Why not? There's more space up there," I say

"But Chris has only just got his certificate for swimming a width." Says Harry.

"He's no need to come," I reply.

So into the deep end we go but after a few minutes there's drama. Lying on the bath side is a body with lots of people crowding around it. Then an anxious, peremptory tannoy-voice tells us all to get out of the pool and to collect our wire basket of clothes. We queue up patiently but soon there is one unclaimed basket. This must belong to the body.

It's still noisy. Harry puts his mouth to my ear, "Pete says, that lad they pulled out of the water has got trunks on the same as Chris's."

From outside my changing cubicle I manage to look down to catch a glimpse of the body. What a relief! I can see it's definitely NOT Chris Enoch, nothing like him. This boy's face seems very pale and puffy.

Then the tannoy-voice asks if anyone knows of a Michael Enoch.

I freeze with horror, trying to make sense of this. Chris's older brother is called Michael. Why would the officials be asking for Michael?

I go to a very tall police officer who's standing on the corner of the pool near the showers and footbath. I feel so small and hesitant. I try to talk to him but with the still-loud, echo-ey noises, the bobby doesn't hear me. He just stares straight ahead.

His eyes transfixed on infinity; his mind elsewhere. I don't try again. Instead, I get dry, dressed and I'm off on my way home.

My dad is shocked when I tell him the sad news.

"Nip to the paper shop for a loaf, will you? You can tell me more when you return," he says.

As I emerge from the Belmont Terrace ginnel with the loaf under my arm I see a police car outside my house.

"Oh no! This is NOT good news," I think.

As I enter my house there's a policeman stood on the visitor's mat.

"This bobby's here about Christopher Enoch," my dad tells me. Then looking at the officer he asks,

"Is it a fatality?"

"Sadly it is," says the policeman.

And I remember thinking quite clearly: "I don't know what the word "fatality" means but I'm certain it's something very bad.

The policeman then explains how confusion was created because Chris had been wearing his older brother's hand-me-down coat with the name, Michael, sewn in.

The next hour is a complete blank.

Later on I go into Shawland's field to watch a football match. Phil Smith asks me on the touchline if it's true that Chris Enoch is dead? I mumble a reply. It's a glorious day. The June sun is out, the day is hot... but my heart is in my boots.

That night my mam tucks me up in bed, which is quite unusual, and says,

"Oh dear! You've had a very tough day today, love. Try and get some rest." Then she kisses me on the forehead. and I think... if my mam says I've had a tough day then I must have.

The six friends who return home that Saturday lunchtime never talk about that day again. Chris's name is never mentioned.

A few weeks later I see Christopher Enoch in the playground. I can't believe it. He's returned to us. My heart leaps with joy. Wow! People CAN return after death. I run towards Chris and spin him round but it's another lad... same size, same shape, same clothes.

I'm totally crestfallen.

Now many years later I do realise that after terrible incidents like this, sometimes good things emerge. Chris's death actually led to certain new health and safety laws: Qualified lifeguards have now to be present at public swimming sessions; the number of bathers is limited at any one time; and much stricter rules about behaviour around the pool side are introduced.

So never allow anyone to get away with moaning about health and safety regulations. Please tell them the story of Christopher Enoch and how his unnecessary death led to a change in the H and S laws and the saving of many other lives.

WHO WAS CHRISTOPHER ENOCH?

Chris was extremely clever. He and his family lived up Dodworth Road just above where Polar Garage used to be. Chris and I were in Miss Plews's class together at Racecommon Road Infants and in Mrs Monkman's class at Agnes Road Junior School for Boys. We were streamed for the first two years at Agnes Road and Chris was not only in the 'A Stream' but always in the Top Row. Chris was an absolute certainty to pass to the grammar school.

He was very sporty and stood out as a footballer, cricketer and athlete. He represented the school at all three activities even though he was only in his penultimate year at junior school. Just before he died I remember our Deputy Head, Mr Bates, taking Chris and myself out onto the bottom playground for a race to determine who should run in the school relay team. I was pretty nippy but Chris, with his long, powerful legs, won quite easily.

Chris was friendly and popular. He had lots of mates. Every year he invited me to his birthday party. After most parties you left with a goody-bag of cake, party blowers, balloons, twizzles and things like that. From Chris's you emerged with an expensive gift like a fountain pen and propelling pencil set.

I think it would be fair to say Christopher had been lucky to come from such a loving, generous family.

Life can be so bloody unfair.

Christopher Enoch, at the age of seven

CHAPTER SIX

HAROLD RUSHFORTH – The head teacher who makes a difference

Harold Rushforth is the head teacher of Agnes Road Junior School for Boys when I start there as a seven year old in 1961. I've never actually met him before although I'm told he's my Nannan Steele's sister's lad, making him my nannan's nephew, and my dad's cousin.

Mr Rushforth is quite a fearsome character, in total charge of our school and it seems almost every other significant activity in life. He's not particularly tall but he's extremely strong and tough and in this he takes a huge pride. His forearms are as thick as men's thighs.

Mr Rushforth's calendar is always full. He plays an important role in the local Labour Party and in Barnsley Football Club; he's the Secretary of Barnsley National Union of Teachers; he's in charge of Barnsley Schools' football, cricket, swimming, and athletics; and is involved with the church - running the Drama Group at St Paul's, Old Town. However, he somehow seems to still find time to do 101 other activities. His genius at organising, means he's able to undertake twice the workload of most ordinary people.

Mr Rushforth's a superb teacher and head teacher who cares just as much for the poor kids as he does the rich, and just as much for those who struggle with learning as he does the 'gifted'. He makes it his duty to get to know every single pupil in his school, so no one feels isolated. He ensures everyone's given a fair chance to succeed and will have no truck with prejudice of any kind. One of the students at 'Aggy Road' is from a traveller family who live in a caravan on waste land up Pond Street. His class teacher has no respect for ethnic minorities and sometimes makes overt slurs against the lad and his family. Eye-witnesses say the word 'Gypsy' or 'Gypo' is sometimes uttered by the boy's class teacher. My mates, in the same class as the traveller-lad, tell me that Mr Rushforth carpets the teacher and threatens him with the sack. I've no idea how they know this but it definitely sounds authentic.

On the occasions that Mr Rushforth has to step in to teach our class, we always feel enriched at the end of the day. He might introduce a classic work of art by, say, LS

Lowry; or a wonderful poem like The Pied Piper of Hamlyn. He might even share a terrific piece of writing by someone from another class; or help us make sense of obscure grammar; or get us to produce a piece of beautiful handwriting that is miraculously and immaculately displayed during lunch break. At a time when many junior schools are narrowing the curriculum and insisting their students undertake endless 11 Plus mock exams, Mr Rushforth insists on broadening it, to include PE, Games, Gymnastics, Music, Art and Craft, Creative Writing, Literature, French, Drama, Science, History, Geography and even boxing and trampolining, et al. Furthermore, despite his less-than conventional stance on the curriculum, Agnes Road's 11 Plus results are always outstanding.

On top of all this, Mr Rushforth can somehow get into your head, in a nice way. He draws attention to the fact that EVERY person has talents and whatever those are, he'll do his damnedest to make sure they are identified and developed. To achieve this he invites experts in to school to share their knowledge and is forever arranging local, national and even international visits. In short, Mr Rushforth's influence turns his school into a learning centre for us to explore the whole world, including ourselves. Personally, I love every minute of my time at Agnes Road and although I might not shine academically, I adore taking part in all the inter-school sports and regular school concerts. Agnes Road Junior School makes everyone feel alive, excited and a 'somebody'.

However, one thing you don't dare do with Mr Rushforth, no matter who you are, is to get on the wrong side of him. In the summer of 1964 our school party is walking along a packed and sunny promenade in Blankenberge, Belgium. There's about twenty of us including Mr Rushforth and his wife. Walking in the same direction and looking to have some fun are half a dozen rowdy Dutch lads, in their mid to late teens. One of them has a miniature pirate's gun, that's all the rage. The gun explodes caps which make a cracking noise, but this particular gun uses caps that create a terrific bang and give off the pungent smell of cordite. One hooligan decides to put his pistol to the ear of Geoff Humphries who's walking beside me and Rob Rookledge. The blast is so loud, Rob and I jump a mile. The pirate turns away proud of his 'assault'. Geoff is in pain and tears. The next sixty seconds will stay recorded in my memory forever:

It takes Mr Rushforth about two seconds to assess the situation. Suddenly, like Oddjob in the film Goldfinger, he moves niftily into the middle of the hooligans with the culprit in his sights. Two on the outer-ring are knocked skittling as Mr Rushforth grabs the guilty one by the ear and pulls him to the ground, while eye-balling his mates. They look on, terrified, and the young man with the twisted ear is screaming to be released. None of us doubt that if the Dutch lads do collectively fight back, Mr Rushforth will be the last man standing. He then drags the hooligan by his ear to apologise to Geoff Humphries and soon the drama is over and everyone feels safe. He's so tough I'd back him to beat Muhammad Ali and Sonny Liston, put together – with a blind fold on.

Another thing you learn early at Agnes Road is never to try and beat Mr Rushforth in a dispute. In 1964 and '65 he helps create the best under 11s football team in Barnsley. We play sixteen games all season and only suffer one defeat, even though we lose one of our greatest players, Chris Enoch, when he's tragically drowned. The team stays the same throughout the season but at one point Mr Rushforth decides he wants to try and play a lad who, hitherto, has not featured in the school team. This arouses insecurity in the minds of the regular players. Is Mr Rushforth trying to break up the team? We all cross our names off the team sheet to send the message that we're not happy. Mr Rushforth calls a team meeting.

"I've noticed none of you want to play in the friendly match I've arranged" he says, calmly. "Well, that's your decision. But if you do drop-out, I'll make sure our school team also drops out of both league and cup competitions. Your season, therefore, will come to an abrupt end, gentlemen."

I look around at the other lads. We've all known Mr Rushforth for nearly four years so we're convinced that once he's made his mind up, he'll NEVER change it, no matter what.

"Now then" he continues, "when I call your name out, if you want to be permanently deleted from the school team, just answer 'yes' or 'no'."

Gulp! I can see this is going to end badly. Something must be done.

"Mr Rushforth" I say, tentatively raising my hand to speak. "Our problem is this: If we win Holy Rood in this friendly, we're all scared it'll lead to the breakup of our successful team."

Incredibly, Mr Rushforth quickly seizes on the chance to make a useful teaching point at this most inopportune time: "No, Ronnie Steele. Your grammar is incorrect. You can't win Holy Rood. Anything you win, can be taken home and put on your mantelpiece, like a trophy. I can't see you keeping the Holy Rood football team on your mantelpiece, can you? I think you mean, if you 'beat' Holy Rood. "

As I shake my head I can't resist smiling at such a ridiculous thought of the Holy Rood team standing on my mantelpiece at home, especially when I hear a titter of laughter from my mates. Although, I do notice, Mr Rushforth is definitely not smiling.

"Ronnie Steele? Are you playing for us or not?" he says without looking up. I notice his reading glasses are perched on the end of his nose as he licks his pen nib before writing on the team sheet. There's a long pause. He's also sticking out his tongue involuntarily, which is something he always does when he's concentrating hard.

Jesus! If I say 'Not playing' I'll miss our Cup Final on Oakwell against St Helen's Junior. There'll be no second chance and that's a game I've been literally dreaming about for weeks. There's no way I can miss it. So I decide not to fight Mr Rushforth; after all, it would be suicidal – we'd be certain to lose. David beating Goliath hardly ever happens in real life.

"Playing!" I shout, a lot louder than I intended, and there's an audible sigh of relief from all the others. Some pat me on the back or awkwardly shake my hand, like only school boys can do. Soon all the others follow suit and agree to the head teacher's temporary changes. We can all trust Mr Rushforth. He's in charge but let's face it, he never lets anyone down.

A few weeks later, he organises one of the most exciting evenings of all time. He invites one of the greatest cricketers in the world to our school to give a public lecture about his career and to show photo-slides. On that evening, Phil Sharpe, the Yorkshire and England opener, and considered by many as the finest slip fielder in the world, has to fight his way through a crowd of autograph hunters to reach his seat at the front. It's a most informative evening until we reach the Question and Answer session. At first, Phil answers questions about his favourite players, his career successes, and his school education. Then, Garry Blake raises his hand.

"Mr Sharpe. You're known as possibly the finest slip fielder in the world, so can you give us any tips on catching?" says Gary, as all the room spontaneously applaud such a pertinent question.

"Thank you for that" says Phil. "It is a fundamental question" and then he demonstrates how to position his hands: His forearms are almost horizontal and his hands are cupped together as though he's catching water from a tap. "This is how it's done" he adds. Then it's time for another question but Phil is interrupted by Mr Rushforth who is standing at the back.

Mr Rushforth gives a little chuckle, as he usually does when he's ready to argue the toss over anything, and says, "That's not particularly good advice to give to budding cricketers."

"I think I know what I'm talking about" replies the best slip-catcher in the world.

Mr Rushforth gives his view on how to catch a ball, by cupping his hands and pointing all his digits to the ceiling with his thumbs together. Then we have ten minutes of pure embarrassment. We're all like spectators at a tennis match, listening to one argument countering another. But it turns into an intense row. Phil Sharpe is getting angry and frustrated, which you can tell by the tone of his voice but Mr Rushforth isn't. He'll argue the toss till the cows come home with not a hint of irritation or blushing. He's also quite prepared to row in front of an audience. In the end Phil gives in and Mr Rushforth triumphs. It's not Mr Rushforth's finest hour but I don't half envy how he sticks to his guns and cares little for what others think of him. Mr Rushforth is a great man to have on your side and I actually think in this instance he does have a good point.

Mr Rushforth's other great ambition in life, besides educating youngsters, is to toughen them up. If there's one quality in a person he dislikes it's being wimpish. He tells the cricket team more times than I care to remember that we don't need pads or sausage gloves for protection from a rock-hard corkie. Waving a cricket bat in the air, he shouts, "This is all you need for protection. A cricket bat!" And then he tells Arnie Sidebottom to try and bowl him out. Now Arnie Sidebottom (The future England fast bowler) can bowl extremely quickly, even at eleven years old, and every ball is on a perfect length, but Mr Rushforth keeps batting away each delivery without glove or pad-protection. Eventually, Arnie knocks Mr Rushforth's stumps over but the point has been forcefully made: Be brave enough to tackle anything.

Is Mr Rushforth successful in toughening us all up? I can only speak for myself. I don't believe it really makes me a 'harder' person but it certainly forges in me an outward, stiff-upper-lip appearance, which henceforth I display to the world*.

When boys at school have a fall-out and fight he usually offers each of them a pair of school boxing gloves so they can express their anger in the ring. Many a life-time friendship is created this way. I'm always involved in competitive sports so I often seem to be fighting someone or other. However, Mr Rushforth reaches the end of his tether one day after discovering me and the cock-of-the-school, Jeff Milner, have been scrapping, but instead of getting out the gloves he gets out the cane. We each get two painful whacks on the hand. Ouch! It doesn't half hurt but I have no sense of injustice because times were different then. To me it's fair treatment. We knew the rules. I also decide it's wise not to let-on to my parents about my punishment. Anyway, I'd only get the usual homily about learning to lose with grace.

AFTERWORD:

Most boys I talk to, who attend Agnes Road Junior School, agree that the education they receive is first class and a lot of this is down to the skill and dedication of Harold Rushforth. His philosophy is not totally implemented overnight. However, by September 1964 after a number of years as head, all classes at Agnes Road are changed to mixed ability, as 'streaming' is phased out. He's also very influential in campaigning for Comprehensive Education and, consequently, argues fervently against the existence of secondary modern education, for so-called school failures.

Writing this honest history, warts and all, is my chance to let the world know what a wonderfully strong and progressive character Harold Rushforth really was. Born at the beginning of World War One, he was a product of his time and I'm certain he wasn't correct in everything he believed in or did. It's true, he could be a wee bit 'brusson'** at times, but he was without doubt, a powerful force for 'good' and although I never once meet him in a social setting, his influence on me as a person, and later as a school teacher, is huge.

Today, if I hear someone criticise my former head teacher, I suddenly find myself turning into Harold Rushforth, and I can't seem to back down until the argument's won.

I was lucky.

We were lucky.

Harold Rushforth made a significant difference to the lives of many.

* Years later, Mr Rushforth publicly praises my football skills and character in an article in the Sheffield Star, Green 'Un, thus:

"Ronnie Steele [is] small but... will tackle anything. Clever ball control". [Maybe this proves Mr Rushforth did make me tougher after all,]

**'Brusson' is a local word meaning, bossy.

Agnes Road swimming champs

CHAPTER SEVEN

THE REAL BRIAN GLOVER - Summer 1966

It's the summer of '66. Paperback-Writer and Sunny Afternoon dominate the pop charts. The whole nation is buzzing at the thought of the forthcoming World Cup tournament to be staged for the first and only time in England. However, the focus of many students at Longcar Central School is on Scout Dyke Outdoor Education Camp. Everyone's thrilled at the idea of spending five whole school days there on a residential trip.

We're lucky enough to have Mr. Glover as teacher-in-charge. He is firm but very popular because he gives respect to all those who show him the same.

On the first night we're all dead excited. No one gets to sleep before 4 am. After lights-out at 10.30 there is much horse-play: Most lads are talking or running around or pretending to be ghosts or farting or jumping on somebody else's bed or visiting the toilets or sneaking a sprig of holly (smuggled in as contraband) into someone else's bed. There's a ghostly echo in the long corridors; the sound of distant doors closing and the smell of new paint. Brian Glover and "Ted" Heath, the two male teachers in charge of all 60 boys, come in and give us the "Scarborough Warning". Later Mr Glover tries to surprise us. He rattles the brass door knob of our dormitory, enters, and moves quickly to flick on the light switch. By the time the room is lit up, the half dozen or so boys out of their beds have scurried back under the nearest blankets or hidden out of view behind the bed dividing-walls. It reminds me of a scene from The Great Escape when German soldiers search the prisoners' hut and the inmates have seconds to hide evidence of the escape tunnel. On this occasion Mr Glover threatens to dump Keith and his mattress out in the corridor if he can't behave. Keith is soon out in the corridor. Another lad, lying quietly in bed, complains he's missing home.

Mr Glover has organised all students into groups of 10. They are single-sex groups of mixed ages, between 11 and 16 years old. These groups have no adults to act as marshals. So we are to be sent out, on our own, to investigate this unfamiliar, rural environment. Mr Glover makes it clear that our conduct is our own personal responsibility. This is very different to the way things are run back at school. There, the head, Mr Hopkins, rules by violence and has not the slightest faith or trust in any person of any age. I know Mr Glover's ethos could prove risky if things go wrong but the atmosphere at Scout Dyke Camp feels a whole lot better than school. It's liberating.

On Tuesday morning our group leaves the Centre with one route map and a compass. It's gloriously sunny without a breath of wind. We're assigned the Gunthwaite Walk with the 'brief' to "stick to the route and explore anything of interest and report back". We chat with friends but we're also on the lookout for something worth "writing home about". Someone spots a large stone gatepost in the middle of a field with nothing around it. Strange. Why a gatepost on its own, slap bang in the middle of a field? We try to make sense of it. It has huge, rusty hinge pegs that must have been forged when the peasants were revolting?!? Maybe this massive stone post had a fence or hedge or gate attached to it many hundreds of years ago? Hmmm... I now notice WE are asking all the questions and no one feels guilty for not providing answers. On we walk, sticking to the map directions and eventually come across a narrow, noisy brook. Interesting.

We all search for signs of life in the water, especially trout. John, a fifth former and our natural leader, alerts us to the presence of a shy, water-creature, which has disappeared under a large flat pebble. He stands astride, one foot on the bank and one on a large round rock in the middle of the stream. Tilting up the pebble, we see a creature none of us recognise. We all gather round. Soon a few of us, shoeless and sockless and with trouser legs rolled up, are paddling in the cool, clear water but with eyes fixed on the silent creature. I'm sure we've all caught toads, newts, sticklebacks, water-boatmen and pond skaters before, but this little creature... we don't recognise and we're all absolutely fascinated.

"It's a crab" shouts one kid, hitching his specs higher up his nose.

"No, it's a baby lobster," says another and everyone laughs.

John has him between his thumb and first finger and places him gently into my flat, upturned palm. I'm one of the youngest and this makes me feel important. My hands are small but this little beauty doesn't even cover it. Everyone's really excited.

"Does anyone know what it is? Its name, like?" asks John.

"Aye. It's called Fred," some wag shouts.

Back in school that would have warranted a telling-off or more probably a terrifying trip to see the tyrannical Mr Hopkins for a dose of the cane.

We spend a short time observing Fred. We all notice his dark brown shell and the yellowy-white underside. Also, he's got two waving antennae, like a Dr Who monster, and a pair of relatively large and menacing pincer-claws. He seems to be aware he's under intense scrutiny. And it's true, he does look a bit like a cross between a miniature crab and lobster.

John lovingly returns Fred to his home under the pebble. We're all dying to discover his proper name as we continue on our circular walk.

Back at Camp, Messrs Glover and Heath are as excited about our find as we are. After a shower and evening meal our group races up to the library to thumb through the reference books. Oh what joy and triumph we feel when we find a picture of Fred. Our shy creature is identified as a crayfish and this is the time of year they mate and give birth. I'm feeling all enriched and satisfied. Apart from the Daily Mirror sports pages and Football Annuals this is the first time I realise how useful books can be. Mr Glover suggests we find out more and perhaps make sketches with labels so students from other schools can appreciate our findings. Wow! That's sounds brilliant! After all, our only audience back at school is the teacher, whose job it is to judge and grade using red ink. But here we're preparing our work for a real, authentic audience. I soon see that the completed drawings and written explanations are amazingly accomplished and there's no one watching over us telling us to try harder or do things differently. It's inspiring working alongside older, more skilful students. All the decisions are ours. We have total responsibility for the quality of our efforts. Suddenly we all become perfectionists and we just love it.

This day is a seminal lesson for me. In one short informal session, Mr Glover and Mr Heath have shown us the secret of learning for pleasure, self-motivation, group interaction, mutual respect, personal responsibility and the absolute thrill of research and discovery.

By the end of the week the display boards in the foyer, outside the main Camp hall, are full of the most outstanding work. I'm fairly certain Miss Atkinson, head of the school Art Department and in charge of the girls here at Scout Dyke, is responsible for this. For the first time in our lives at secondary school, apart from success on the school football field, many of us feel a genuine sense of collective, student pride.

I can't for the life of me think why, back at school, nothing comes anywhere near this. Maybe it's because teachers like Brian Glover are almost as oppressed and powerless as we are?

Looking back now I'm convinced the real Brian Glover was very much aware of modern teaching methods and confident he could make them work. His educational philosophy was clear: "Young people are candles to be lit, not vessels to be filled."

54 years later, my best mate from school, Ged Wilcock, sends me this message:

"I wasn't in the group that found the crayfish that day but remember, clearly, the excitement and interest it generated that night back in the hall. Also, the motivation we had the following days to discover something that might equal or better it. You are right, it really was something special and, while I didn't realise it at the time, Brian Glover was able to nurture our desire to learn more. Marvellous!"

Brian Glover our soccer coach.
I'm sat with the ball at my feet.

CHAPTER EIGHT

BORN LUCKY

Some people are just born lucky and I guess I'm one of them. Throughout my whole life I've always sailed close to the wind, have taken too many risks without always considering the consequences, but somehow just managed to avoid serious trouble - but only by the skin of my teeth.

It's 1966 and I'm a twelve year-old student at Longcar Central Selective Secondary School near Locke Park. The day gets off to a disastrous start when me and Andy Watson are tussling to get control of a small rubber ball as we play football on the school drive. Every so often we have to suspend our game when teachers drive past to reach the school car park. At one point we hear a car horn pip and look up to see Miss Pool's* Mini Cooper, speeding towards us, so we both have to nip out of the way, sharpish. I manage to jump clear but Miss Pool's front tyre runs over Andy's right heel. I can tell the car's caught him by the way the front end jumps slightly, like it's run over a large pebble. Andy can hardly walk. Miss Pool knows she's gone too far this time so she stops her car with a screech of the brakes and gets out.

Miss Pool is an overweight 50 year old who's always looking for a scapegoat for her unfulfilled time on earth. She knows she's in the wrong here so her tone is markedly softer than usual.

"I don't think the car quite touched you, did it?" she says, as she inspects her tyre to make sure there's no damage to her precious vehicle.

"It just clipped me, Miss. It's nothing really. I'll be okay in a minute" says Andy, trying to put his weight on his foot and falling over.

"Well, you boys shouldn't be on the driveway at all, should you? And you were flouting school rules by playing football. But I'll overlook it this time" she says, climbing back into her car and zooming off like a villain being chased by the cops.

I feel so angry. Every day Miss Pool speeds like a maniac up that drive. Male students** have to negotiate it to reach the playground but this rarely causes any problems. However, Miss Pool is always scattering groups of lads whose only wish is to live long enough to hear the school bell ring... and then she's turns it round to blame on us. The cheek!

"You know what she is, don't you?" I say to Andy. "She's what you call a bastard." And I find actually uttering those words makes me feel better and I see they also make Andy smile through his pain.

Today is Monday and I hate Mondays more than ever. The first two lessons are okay because it's double Science with Mr Whitney and though he is a fearsome character, I love the way he teaches Physics. However, my heart sinks when I think of having Miss Pool for double Geography after morning break. This doesn't just spoil my Mondays for a whole year, it even spoils my weekends because by Saturday night I'm already dreading Monday coming round again.

Physics that day turns out to be a great lesson. Mr Whitney proves to us that hot water rises and cold water sinks using a glass beaker full of water, a bunson burner, tripod and some wood shavings. He also shows us how to convert centigrade to Fahrenheit and vice versa, using a simple mathematical formula which stays with me for the rest of my life. Then he asks us why today is a very special day.

Ged Wilcock puts up his hand. He's clever is Ged. "Is today special because it's the anniversary of D-Day, Sir?"

"Oh, well done Young Man. Give that boy a dog biscuit" says Mr Whitney and everyone laughs. "But that is NOT the answer I'm looking for. The answer I am looking for is something to do with dates and numbers."

Dave Riddiough puts his hand up this time.

"Yes?" says Mr Whitney. He can't say "Yes, Riddiough or yes Wilcock" because even after teaching us for a year he's not bothered to learn anyone's name. In fact not many teachers at Longcar go to the trouble of learning our names. Perhaps it's school policy. Maybe the head teacher thinks that if they call students' by their name they might all turn out to be serial killers or something.

"Is it something to do with the numbers that make up today's date, all being 6's, Sir?" says Dave Riddiough.

"By golly he's got it" says Mr Whitney and he writes on the blackboard:

"6/6/66"

"I want you all to appreciate this" says Mr Whitney "because it happens very rarely. And I'll tell you one other thing before the bell goes for break time: The number six means 'to flow and make progress' in Chinese and so the number 6 is regarded as a lucky number by many. So if you believe in lucky 6, expect good fortune today."

On the playground at break, Andy Watson is still limping. "Just think, if the number six really brought you luck, Andy, you could have been laid up in hospital, eating grapes, instead of looking forward to double Geography with laugh-a-minute, Miss Pool."

"Oh, Ronnie, just shurrup can't you? I'm not in the mood. My heel is killing me" he says and I feel so sorry for him I offer him a Golden Wonder from my half-empty packet.

In Geography, Miss Pool has an expression on her face that's even more sour than usual. She sees Andy hobble into her room but doesn't bother asking how he is. Her mind's on other things. She always spends the first five minutes of each lesson ranting on about something or other. Sometimes it's about those scroungers who are unemployed, or those "idiots who vote Labour only because their parents voted that way". Today, however, she expresses her disdain for adults who waste their money on alcohol, cigarettes and bingo. It's an old familiar refrain and every time she mentions it, I feel annoyed because it sounds like she's talking about my mam and dad: after all, they both enjoy the occasional drink, smoke Park Drive unfiltered and go to the bingo once or twice a week, but at least they're happy, funny, kind and hardworking. Whereas, Miss Pool is none of those things. After five minutes of her ranting I feel I can't take anymore but I'm not suicidal. If I told Miss Pool to shut her poisonous gob up, I imagine the head and deputy would soon get to know, and then they'd thrash me in assembly while everyone in school watches, like those public executions you see in history books. Okay, my imagination might exaggerate the consequences a bit but not by much. Nope, the truth is, open rebellion at Longcar Central is definitely not an option.

Miss Pool's five minutes is not quite up so she continues: "I'm convinced there are thousands of people out there, smoking and drinking and gambling and then complaining that they have too little money. They're disgusting" she says and twists her face even more on the word 'disgusting' just for effect. "If it was up to me I'd ban smoking and gambling and make theatre-going compulsory.

"Tell me" she adds as a finale "how many of your parents go to the theatre? It wouldn't surprise me if the answer is 'none'. Dear me! Sometimes I despair!"

Miss Pool really is a snobby bastard.

I'm so mad I put up my hand without even knowing what I'm going to say.

"What do YOU want?" she snaps.

"I want to tell you that my mam and dad enjoy the theatre each week" I say, sounding like the posh child of middle-class intellectuals.

"What? Do you mean your parents go to the cinema? She asks, studying my face to see whether I'm winding her up.

"Yes, my parents go to the cinema but they also go to the theatre, Miss Pool."

"And tell me" she says "Do your parents also chew gum when they go to the theatre?"

Oh no, she's spotted me chewing a piece of Beechnut. It's a fair cop so I walk to the basket and drop it in.

"And I'll expect 200 lines tomorrow saying 'I must not chew gum in class'."

By now I'm not just angry, I'm blazing. Miss Pool has nothing but contempt for all of us including our parents and that's when I make the daddy of all mistakes. As I sit down at my desk near the back, I open up the shiny new text book in front of me and write in ink:

"Miss Pool is a bastard"

However, even before the blue ink is dry I begin to regret it. I especially regret not even altering my handwriting style. But it's too late because the deed is already done and nothing can undo it. Oh dear, my temper doesn't half get me into some pickles. I'll need some luck to get out of this one.

As we walk out of the Geography classroom at the end of the lesson, Valerie White whispers, "Ey up, Ronnie Steele. When does *your* mam and dad go to the theatre?"

"Every Wednesday" I say nonchalantly. "You know the old Theatre Royal on Wellington Street? It's been converted into a bingo joint now."

After lunch, Ian Moran from another first year class opens up his text book, sees it's been defaced by some 'no-mark' and takes it to show Miss Pool. Many in the class report that, at first, Miss Pool goes purple with fury but then starts to work-out when this outrage was perpetrated. They are brand new text books so it must have been done that morning. At afternoon break time everyone in our class is ordered to line up outside Miss Pool's room. Word has already got round to all my classmates that it was me who defaced the book so I fully expect to be 'shopped' by someone. Besides, surely Miss Pool remembers me trying to wind her up. This is getting serious and I'm starting to think of all the worst consequences. It'll be the cane followed by a 'shaking of the heads' by all those teachers I love and respect. I'll be really upset if I'm a disappointment to the teachers I admire. Then, of course, there'll be expulsion from school and the end of my football career even before it's started. It's the football thing more than anything else that makes me feel like rooaring***.

When Miss Pool turns up she sits us down and hands out a sheet of paper to everyone. She never says what the problem is but just instructs us to write our own name plus "Miss Pool". Of course, in order to throw her off the scent I disguise my handwriting and use a different pen. But I'm scared. Very scared. How long before someone cracks? or some sycophant looks to gain 'creep points' by acting as class informant?

When I think about it all, Miss Pool is really dumb not to look through everyone's Geography exercise book in order to identify the guilty one. However, I'm forgetting that she's probably too lazy to spend an hour combing through books.

It doesn't take Miss Pool long to identify the culprit. She compares Rob Sherriff's handwriting with that in the book and is convinced he's done it and I can guess why. Rob went to the same primary school as me and was taught the same italic script. Miss Pool makes the allegation and cross-examines Rob but gets nowhere. Rob of course is innocent and knows I did it, so it must be tempting for him to say, "It wasn't me but I do know who's responsible."

When Rob reaches the playground he tells me not to worry. "I'm no grass, Ronnie. She can never prove I did it and she knows it. Besides you know what her problem is, don't you?" says Rob with both his hands stuffed in his pockets. "Miss Pool wants to keep this quiet. She's desperate that other teachers never find out that her students can't abide her."

Rob Sherriff is another brain box.

Phew! What a relief! If Rob Sherriff had been punished for my misdemeanour I would have had no choice but to stand up and own up. I couldn't possibly have lived with seeing someone else punished for what I'd done. However, nothing more is ever said about the incident and the whole thing soon blows over and is forgotten.

What a day 6/6/66 was for me. My entire world could have fallen apart had it not been for the strength of character of Rob Sherriff. That, and maybe I was just born lucky.

* Some names have been changed to avoid embarrassment.

**At Longcar the boys and girls had a separate drive and playground.

*** "Rooaring" is a local Barnsley word meaning "weeping".

CHAPTER NINE

OUR VERY FIRST LESSON WITH MR HINES – September 1966

Kes author, Barry Hines, is teaching at Longcar Central School when he writes his most famous novel.

It's September 1966 and England have just been crowned Football Champions of the World! National euphoria has infected everyone, male and female, young and old. The Beach Boys, with God Only Knows, are riding high in the Pop Charts and everyone seems to be playing or singing it. The early autumn weather is pleasant for the students at Longcar Central School and today we have our new PE teacher, Mr Hines, for Games for the first time.

We know very little about him but many accomplished sportsmen in our year are desperately hoping Mr Hines is a good, conscientious teacher. Melv Henighan hears that he's had a book published about the life of an aspiring, professional footballer, so he borrows it from the public library and shows us some of the racy extracts at break-time. I still love comic strips like Roy of the Rovers so I plan to borrow it when Melv's done with it. I've already seen Mr Hines walking to school wearing his unbuttoned, black, duffle coat, carrying a rucksack and I'm shocked at his youthfulness. I once actually mistake him for a pupil. I notice he's always immaculately turned out in fine tracksuit and trainers when inside school. I also hear the girls gossiping about this 'gorgeous new teacher'.

When we're all changed and on the playground he lines us up so we can get organised into teams. The smell of burning wood is drifting over the playground, from the allotment gardens. Mr Hines doesn't pick teams in the traditional way where the two best players take turns to pick the best footballers until only the humiliated are left. Instead, he gives a letter to the first four boys in the line: A, B, C, D and stands them apart from the rest of us.

"You four are captains of each team," he says. Then to the rest of us: "I'm going to give you a letter. If you are an A you stand behind the A captain. B, stand behind the B captain, and so on. And he then goes down the long line of kids, tapping individuals on the shoulder saying, A, B, C, D; A, B, C, D, until we have four teams of seven players. The teams have been picked at random in less than two minutes and no one's made to feel embarrassed just because they're not gifted. Hmmm... I love his technique. It's smart, kind, efficient and fair.

"These are the four teams you'll be in, for football, for the rest of this half-term," he says as he sticks his chin out like someone wearing an uncomfortable collar and tie. I also notice he has a habit of stretching his left arm slightly when he talks, like people do when their sleeve feels too long. This is a quirk of nature I notice more and more about Mr Hines but I never mention it and no one else flags it up, ever. We might take the rise out of unpleasant teachers but not those who are fair. Anyway, he's that sharp, if you tried it on, he could make you look pretty silly, rather quickly, I think.

"I'll be publishing results and league tables each week", says Mr Hines, moving his chin and neck slightly. We're all dead impressed with this and I think... he really does sound interested in us and excited about what he does.

"Right captains, pick the name of a Scottish Second Division Club and you'll keep that name until half-term", says Mr Hines.

"We'll be Morton" says our captain, Heppy, looking down our line of players for some reassuring thumbs-up. Good choice. Morton are top of the Scottish Second Division. Then Mr Hines stuffs his whistle and red braid into his hip pocket and from his other he takes out a biro, a piece of paper and jots down the team names.

"Does anyone know the stadium where Morton play their home games?" asks Mr Hines, taking off his specs and letting them hang on pieces of thread. Dave Riddiough puts his hand up.

"They play at Cappielow, Sir," answers Dave.

For a split second Mr Hines looks flabbergasted. "Cappielow? Cappielow. Yes, yes, Cappielow" he says, clearing his throat. "Of course I knew that all along" he says but he finds it impossible to keep a straight face and most of us get the joke. "Well done, lad!" And we're all super-impressed with Dave's encyclopaedic knowledge of British football grounds.

"In that case," says Mr Hines, "Morton will be playing Hamilton Academicals in their Second Division home fixture here at the Cappielow Stadium, while I take

Stenhousemuir and Raith Rovers onto the grass where I've set up a football skills circuit. Oh and by the way, the ref's not turned up. Let's say he's stuck in traffic somewhere, so you'll have to referee the game yourselves. And don't be falling out".

I can't believe what's just happened. In less than five minutes we've got teams picked for the whole half-term and we're already kicking-off on the tarmac playground – also known as Cappielow Stadium – while Mr Hines takes the other half of the class for skills practice.

The rest of the lesson goes smoothly except for one incident where Mr Hines's genius emerges. My team, Morton, are leading Hamilton Academicals one-nil when a shot goes in off the post (a traffic cone). It should be 2 – 0 but a big, noisy row ensues. Hamilton players fiercely contest the goal. Nobody will back down because we're almost all bad losers. Insults are bawled out! Fists are clenched.

Leaving his skills group, Mr Hines calmly tells us all to find a space and sit down. The skills group also pause their dribbling and football-juggling activities, just to be nosey.

"Riddiough," he says. "What's happening?"

"We scored a good goal, Sir and the Hamilton Academicals lot say it hit the post".

"And did it hit the post, Riddiough?" asks Mr Hines.

"It did, Sir but it bounced off and went in the goal."

Without a trace of impatience in his voice, Mr Hines says, "Well it's up to you fourteen boys to sort this out. I told you earlier, you're all referees today. Now you can spend the next ten minutes sat down getting a beautiful sun tan or you can sort it out yourselves and carry on with your game" and he turns round and heads back to the football-jugglers.

Desperate not to waste playing-time, we accept it's not a goal and the dispute is immediately resolved. Later I think, how clever this was of Mr Hines. He didn't increase the tension or resort to threats. Instead, like the King Solomon I heard about at junior school, he provides a quick, acceptable solution.

Half way through the lesson Morton and Hamilton Academicals swap activities with Stenhousemuir and Raith Rovers but before he blows the whistle for their second kick-off, Mr Hines makes an announcement:

"From now on, even if a shot only brushes the inside of the post on its way into goal, it is NOT to be counted as a goal. It's a goal-kick instead. That clear everyone?" We all nod even though we're not altogether convinced about his logic. It's weeks before we all accept that the rule change does indeed lead to many fewer disputes.

Back in the changing room Mr Hines makes another announcement:

I'd like a quick word with you, you and you." He points to me, Melv Henighan and Alan Newsam.

"You three are Steele, Henighan and Newsam. That right?", he asks, reading our names from a scrap of paper.

"Yes, Sir", we chorus.

"Don't forget your boots tomorrow. The Under-fourteens are playing St Michaels at home and you three are picked".

Wow! I can't believe it. I'm walking on air. I'm so happy. I can't wait to tell my parents. I'm in the team for the year above my age group, again, and I didn't even realise Mr Hines was watching and assessing me. Yes! yes! yes! yes! He's a good eye for talent that Mr Hines, I tell myself.

"Thanks for picking me for the school team, Sir," I say to him with heartfelt gratitude. "I didn't even realise you were watching and judging my performance".

"I wasn't. I asked Riddiough for names of those who played for the Under- 13s last season and he gave me yours", he replies with a mischievous smile and a wink in Dave Riddiough's direction. We all laugh uproariously and Mr Hines has to quieten us. England are world champs, I'm in the school football team, Mr Hines is our teacher and life is so good!

On the way out from the changing room, which is really the school cloakroom, Mr Hines announces his Player of the Day.

"My Player of the Day is", and he pauses for dramatic effect... "Young Sheriff! Chosen because not one of his passes went astray".

Now Rob Sheriff is NOT a footballer. Brilliant at English but at sport, few would describe him as a natural. However, Mr Hines's choice and his reasoning has a magical effect. We're all so pleased for Rob and at the same time we feel a satisfying sense of cooperation and togetherness. Everyone is valued and has something to offer, it seems. And as I leave the finest PE lesson of my life I try to make sense of the whirlwind that is Mr Hines:

He's economical with his praise.

He has the wisdom of King Solomon.

He has the same value for tryers as he does for potential super-stars.

He's fair.

He makes you laugh.

He gives respect to those who earn it.

He seems to value everyone.

Melv Henighan

He prefers small-sided games so there's lots of involvement. He can motivate without wheedling, bribing, bullying, beating, shouting or punishing.

Yes, our very first PE lesson with Mr Hines was certainly one to remember.

Dave Riddiough today

CHAPTER TEN

BARRY HINES AND HIS HILARIOUS ONE-LINERS – Spring 1967

It's the Autumn Term of 1967 at Raley Secondary Modern, Barnsley. The world is changing for the better. The Summer of Love has passed and the UK government has just made homosexuality legal. Furthermore, after years of campaigning and many thousands of unnecessary deaths and imprisonments, a law is passed in Parliament to legalise abortion. Prime Minister Harold Wilson's image, in the nude, has been controversially used by the pop band, The Move, for sales promotion. Barry Hines is spending most of his spare time trying to finish off his new novel about a boy and a kestrel. He hopes to get it published as early as possible in the New Year but he hasn't got a title for it yet.

Paul Wilkinson loves PE and Games, partly because he's an accomplished athlete but also because he greatly admires his part-time teacher, Barry Hines. At this moment in time Barry is teaching at no less than three different secondary schools: Raley, Longcar and St Helen's. Paul thinks Mr Hines is so very different to any other teacher he's ever come across. His rapport with students is unmatched and he doesn't feel his control is threatened by a bit of cheeky banter. Mr Hines is quick-witted enough to counter it with ease and make everyone laugh with his one-liners.

As Mr Hines sets up two small football pitches using cones and skittles, he appoints Paul to do a follow-my-leader warm-up session with the rest of the class. As Paul performs three press-ups the other 29 students simply copy him. Then it's star-jumps, windmill arms-spins, burpees, etc. Anyone watching would notice that a ginger-haired lad is a tiny bit slower than the others, his timing a fraction out. As the boys gradually loosen up, loud radio music is heard coming from a red-bricked semi just behind the tall perimeter fence. A couple of workmen are replacing an old back door and the boys laugh when they hear the worst vocalist in the history of the world, singing at the top of his voice:

"I'm just sitting watching flowers in the rain

Feel the power of the rain

Watching the garden grow."

Instead of hearing Paul's instructions all they can hear is The Voice, who's so off-key it makes their eyes water. When Mr Hines returns, Paul says, "That singing workman's putting us off, Sir!"

"Singing? is that what you call it?" says Mr Hines. "Thought he'd trapped his hand in the door." Every one laughs in unison except Ginger who laughs when everyone else has finished.

Mr Hines is ready to make an announcement but he has to pause now while the 10:40 Leeds train clickety-clacks its way along the nearby embankment. He clears his throat:

"Brazil are two players down today because of FIFA suspensions, so as they're already bottom of the South American Continental League I'll be playing on their team," says Mr Hines, removing his glasses and putting them into a hard specs-box. The boys smile because they know Brazil are two players short through influenza, not FIFA suspension, but Mr Hines does like to appeal to the imagination. No one quibbles with him taking part today because they're all aware of how poor the Brazil players are.

"Hough... what's a matter with your Brazil shirt today?" asks Mr Hines as he kneels on one knee to fasten a loose lace.

"Aw, my mam's washing it today, sir" replies Mick Hough. Then Paul watches as Mr Hines takes a very small book, like a diary, out of his pocket and writes something in it. Strange.

"What are you writing, sir?" asks Paul, trying to catch sight of the words he's written.

"Aide-memoire, Wilkinson, Aide-memoire. You never know when you're going to need good ideas" he says, closing the diary.

"For your story-writing, Sir?" asks Paul.

"Exactly."

During one of the games, Ian Ward get's lucky. He stands in the way of a defensive clearance and the ball ricochets into the goal.

"That was jammy, Wardie."

"What a fluke!"

"Bet you can't do that again, Wardie!"

But Mr Hines jumps to Ward's defence with: "What are you talking about, jammy? Jammy doesn't come into it. It doesn't matter if you score with your left nostril, as long as it goes in the net." Everyone smiles because Mr Hines has beaten this drum before.

The lesson finishes with a penalty shoot-out competition between Brazil and Argentina. Each player, bar the keeper, takes two penalties.

Mr Hines's Brazil score an enviable nine out of a possible fourteen. Poor, Argentina, miss their first four so the teacher and his players are celebrating early. In the end Brazil win 9 – 8, except they've miscalculated and Argentina have still two more players to shoot.

"What?" says Mr Hines, his veins sticking out on his temple. "Two more penalty takers? Where are you getting them from, Wilkinson, Huddersfield Road?" And Dave Deakin is laughing so hard he has to take three run-ups before he converts the winning kick.

At the end of lesson, Mr Hines monitors those collecting the cones and skittles as the rest of the class head back towards the steep school drive. The workmen are putting in a new window frame now and though the radio is turned off now, The Voice is still blasting it out:

"I'm just sitting watching flowers in the rain

See the power of the rain

Watching the garden grow"

Ginger – real name, Mark Jenkins- is the type who does daft things without thinking, which gets him into loads of trouble. When he first arrived at Raley, he passed Mr Walker, the Woodwork teacher, in the corridor. Now Mr Walker has a bulbous, flaming-red nose and Mark says loudly: "Whooo! Look at his nose!" Walker went mad and poor Jenkins got six of the best even though he'd no idea why. Mark's mam jokes that she must have dropped him on his head when he was a baby because her other two passed to Broadway Grammar. Mark is very likeable but he's just a bit slow, that's all. The odd thing is though, he can tell you the name and birthday of every single scholar at Raley.

He walks over to the criss-cross wire fence.

"Ey up, mister!" he shouts to The Voice through the fence. The Voice stops singing and turns round to listen. Paul and his class mates start to cringe, wondering what Mark will say next. He remembers what Mr Hines said earlier and trots it out verbatim: "I thought you'd trapped your hand in the door!"

The Voice's face drops. He suddenly looks quite annoyed. "You cheeky little... Do you fancy a thick ear?" he asks.

"If you hit me I'll fetch my dad to you" says Mark as usual (He's never known his dad).

"Oh, you will, will you?" says The Voice, "and I'll fetch my dad and he's the heavyweight champion of the world. What's your dad going to do then?" Mark Jenkins looks worried. The thought of the heavy-weight Champion of the World coming up to school scares him no end.

Mr Hines has heard almost everything.

"Jenkins!" shouts, Mr Hines. "If you don't come away from that fence I'll knock you through it and you'll come out like a bag of chips!" The Voice laughs at Mr Hines's words. Mark doesn't fancy becoming a bag of chips.

Addressing The Voice, Mr Hines says, "It's alright. The lad doesn't mean any harm. He's a heart of gold. He just doesn't think things through, that's all."

The Voice's face takes on a more understanding look and he waves a 'thank you' to Mr Hines and returns to singing.

"I'm just sitting..."

Mr Hines rolls his eyes but at least the mini drama is over. However, Mark looks dead miserable so Mr Hines tells him he can tidy up the PE cupboard at break time. Suddenly his face beams like someone from a Colgate-ring-of-confidence advert.

Mr Hines is now scribbling something else in his little diary.

"Another aide-memoire again, sir?" asks Paul.

"Certainly is, Wilkinson. I'm harvesting ideas all the time. Now do me a favour will you? Remind me when we get back in school to phone the police" says Mr Hines.

What? Phone the police, Sir?

"Yes," says Mr Hines, "That workman's been murdering that beautiful song all morning."

Back in the changing room Paul and his mates are giving Mr Hines plenty of stick for losing the penalty competition and now they congregate at the changing room exit, still taunting him. Mr Hines pretends to be angry and shouts, "Get out of my blasted sight" and bounces the football towards them. He throws it harder than intended and it hits a coat-peg and the ceiling, almost smashing the light. That's the students' cue to scarper, laughing all the way down the corridor.

Paul forgets his towel and has to go back. On his way he thinks about all the wonderful times he's enjoyed doing PE with Mr Hines: playing football, cricket, volleyball, gymnastics, pirates etc. What a life it must be, teaching PE. Surely, you don't need to be academic to teach it, do you? Isn't it enough to learn the rules for many different sports?

"Hope you're not back to rub salt in my wounds, Wilkinson" says Mr Hines, as he changes his footwear.

"No Sir. Was just thinking, Sir. What do you have to do to be a PE teacher?"

"You need your English and Maths O' Levels and then you do a three year course at teacher training college" says Mr Hines. Paul's face and shoulders drop a mile and Mr Hines notices the terrible disappointment. However, sadly, it now seems too late to sugar-coat the truth.

"Thank you, Sir" says Paul as he turns, forgets his towel again, and trudges his way to the next lesson.

Next day Paul is told by his form teacher that he has to see Mr Hines in the school library after last lesson. When he gets there Mr Hines is busy composing his new book about a boy and his kestrel. Beside him, on the table, in a very neat pile, is a small collection of books on careers.

"Here you are Paul" says Mr Hines, breaking the age-old Raley school rule and addressing a student by his first name. Paul looks over his shoulder half-expecting Mr Hines to be talking to someone else. "I used these books myself when I was your age. They're excellent."

"Thank you Mr Hines, thank you" says Paul, aware there's a slight tremble in his grateful voice.

A few years later, Paul Wilkinson becomes a very happy and successful, top-class, Barnsley men's hairstylist.

(Thanks in particular to Paul Wilkinson and Ged Wilcock for help and advice with this narrative. Also, almost all names have been changed to protect the guilty)

Paul Wilkinson

CHAPTER ELEVEN

BARRY HINES FACES CLASS REVOLT – February 1967

It's spring 1967. The British steel industry is struggling badly, so Harold Wilson and his Labour government decide to re-nationalise it. The Conservative Party see no alternative and so are in agreement. In March the huge oil tanker, the SS Torrey Canyon, is shipwrecked just off the coast of Cornwall and spills its crude oil, causing an ecological disaster. In April, Muhammad Ali is stripped of his world boxing title and barred from fighting for three years because he says he will not take up arms against the Vietcong. In May, Elvis marries Priscilla and the Beatles release their watershed album, Sergeant Pepper's Lonely Hearts' Club Band.

At Longcar Central School half of our class is in the school gymnasium playing volleyball under the watchful eye of Mr Hines. It's the school assembly hall really but it doubles as a gym. There's also a stage for theatre but for some reason there is no drama group at our school. Shame really.

Today is the climax of a whole half-term playing this fantastic, new sport. Our present game is almost over. It's the final point. We're 24 – 22 down and it's Steve Robson's team to serve. I suspend my concentration for a second or two to capture the whole scene. Through the big hall windows to my left I can see the staffroom but because of the February fog I can't quite make out the boys' playground. Inside the hall there are six of us on each side of the volleyball net and the focus is positively intense. The game has been going for thirty minutes and everyone is dripping with sweat. The slap-on-the-back encouragements are over. Steve prepares to serve. If they win this point it'll mean they win the eight-week-long tournament and our team will be in receipt of the wooden spoon. No one wants that humiliation. There's silence. Steve tosses the red ball into the air and serves a absolute pearler. Then a different Steve – Steve Auden – (our captain) miraculously keeps the ball in play by diving onto his side and scooping the ball up into the air. Paul Sagar keeps it alive brilliantly to set up our star scorer, Les Jones, to smash the ball down for a point. We're saved! Except, two blockers from the other team appear from nowhere, rise up like salmon, present their forearms and bang! the ball rebounds back into our court and hits the parquet floor. It's all over. Robson's

Rulers come top of the league - and Auden's Acrobats are bottom. The Rulers are in ecstasy but our team's reaction is different to anything I've ever known. We hug. We shake hands. We commiserate and a few seconds later we congratulate our opponents. This is very odd behaviour. If my dad had witnessed it he'd have put his hand to my forehead to check that my temperature was normal because usually in defeat I'm ready to argue the toss about anything and everything. However, this time the feeling of pleasure overcomes the disappointment of defeat. It's the same for us all. We've been beaten but still feel good.

Melv Henighan enters the hall, sweating and breathing heavily. He's the first to return from a competitive cross-country run that we are now doing regularly in preparation for an inter-schools competition. As soon as everyone from Melv's half of the class return, we'll swap activities and they'll compete for second and third place in the tournament. In the meantime I've a few minutes to waste so I sit on one of those low, PE benches and do what I'm a superstar at: I begin to daydream... And my daydream takes me back eight weeks to the late autumn term 1966. We're in the run up to Xmas and although there are no decorations in school we're all dead excited because tonight it's our school Xmas disco party. We've just finished our football lesson when Mr Hines drops this bombshell.

"In the New Year I'll be introducing you all to the beautiful game of volleyball," he says, holding his clipboard to his chest.

This sparks pandemonium.

"Oh no, Sir!"

"Volleyball?

"Who wants to play that?"

"It's what lasses play!"

"But we love football, Sir".

Steve Robson

I even notice Steve Robson slaps his wet shirt down onto the cloakroom bench in disgust, and Steve is known for not demonstrating his feelings.

"Listen", says Mr Hines, stretching his arm out to shorten his sleeve and moving his head to one side as though his shirt collar's too tight. "It's good to spend time on different sports then you'll never get stale. Just give it a chance. You'll see… by February half-term you'll have learnt some new skills and you'll develop an even greater thirst for football".

We all try to reason with him but to no avail. This is a disaster with a capital D. We need a meeting, quick, but it's break time and although half our class will soon be on the school playground, the other half will be up at The House. (The House is the school annexe, about a 150 yard walk from the main building).

We agree to meet at lunchtime, and like Gunpowder Plotters we gather furtively on the playground, by the old air-raid shelters, near where the smokers hide. I'm out of breath because I have to go home for lunch but I make sure I get back in plenty of time. The morning fog has lifted.

Our decision is made quickly and is unanimous: We resolve to speak to Mr Hines and try again to persuade him to change his mind. But no one's volunteering to represent us because it means someone has to fetch him out of the dreaded staffroom. Think I'd sooner try and escape over the Berlin Wall.

"Why don't you do it, Ronnie? He might listen to you," says Steve Carroll, using his fingers to comb his blonde fringe across his forehead.

"Oh aye, and what if, when I knock on the staffroom door, Adolph answers it?" I say, already feeling like I need a trip to the toilet.

"Don't talk wet," replies Cazzy, "Hopkins never goes into the staffroom except to give teachers the cane".

Everybody laughs, except me.

"Reight! I'll do it but I'm not doing it by missen", I say, noticing my anxiety levels are affecting my spoken English.

The rest of the twenty-odd kids suddenly become surprisingly reticent, then I hear a deep voice from the side.

"I'll come".

It's Steve Robson and my life has just been saved. Steve is of average size, of very few words and very little emotion. He rarely gets mad and he never gets scared. Now, no one ever disturbs teachers in the staffroom at Longcar Central School. Not ever. But we're on a vital mission so we 'foolishly' decide to do it and be damned. Getting past the prefects is hard but we manage it and I already know what I'm going to say because I've practiced it in my head. We make our way through the school hall and pause at the door of hell.

"Abandon hope all ye who enter here," mumbles Steve, ominously. I seriously consider saying a prayer but think better of it. We can hear voices coming from inside and a woman's laugh.

I knock... tap, tap, tap but I know it's too soft. No one comes. Oh bloody hell. I take a deep breath and knock again but this time much harder. Too hard. I feel like running away. The door knob rattles, the door opens, and it's Mr Glover's face we see. Oh thank you God! Thank you!

"Erm... me and Steve Robson would erm... "

"Can we speak to Mr Hines, please?" asks Steve, rescuing me.

"Mr Hines. There's a deputation here to see you", says Mr Glover and as he turns sideways I get my first ever look into the mysterious school staffroom. I see clouds of pipe and cigarette smoke; and the smell is appalling, but at least the staff look and sound like real human beings for a change.

Mr Hines walks through the doorway and closes the door behind him. The staffroom noises and smells are both dulled again. I don't think he's too happy about us bothering him at lunchtime and he reiterates his previous arguments. Then he tells us about his training at Loughborough College where, over a three year period, the students had a great time covering a new sport every half-term. I lose focus for a few seconds, thinking, wow, that sounds brilliant. Then I hear his voice once again:

"I guarantee none of you will regret taking part in volleyball for those eight weeks", says Mr Hines. "Anything else?"

"No, Sir. Thank you, Sir".

Me and Robbo return to tell our fellow plotters what's been said. They take it well and tell us they genuinely thought we would both finish up hanging from a cross at the back of the school hall, as a warning to others.

Don's the only kid who continues to be dissatisfied:

He says, "I wish I'd have gone with you now. I'd have told him straight. He wouldn't have flannelled me!"

"Oh really?" I reply, getting my mad up because we all know Don likes to big-note himself. "Well Mr Hines also said if anyone still feels unhappy he'll organise a meeting in the presence of Mr Hopkins.".

The colour drains from Don's face and he starts to mutter, "No, no, if Mr Hines has definitely made his mind up..." and all the lads burst out laughing and Don, realising he's been called out, joins in the fun...

Suddenly, I awake from my reverie and find I'm back in the real world. I'm sat on the same PE bench in the same school gym with a huge smile on my face, hoping no one's spotted it. I never thought I'd feel the way I feel at this moment; and as we get ready for our very challenging cross-country race, I count my blessings...

We now love volleyball even more than football because every point played is thrilling.

If I can't play football for a career I'd love to train as a PE teacher.

Some of my mates who seem not to be wired up properly when playing football, are absolutely superb at volleyball.

Playing only football for the whole year can, indeed, make you stale. Everyone's opinions should be valid.

And I glimpse, but only briefly, that it is possible to lose a game and still enjoy it.

CHAPTER TWELVE

BRIAN GLOVER SAVES MY LIFE – April 1967

It's the late spring of '67 and I'm twelve years and eleven months old. We return to Scout Dyke Outdoor Education Centre for the second time in under a year with almost the same staff as before. It's Wednesday and we're into our third night in Dormitory One. We're having a fabulous time because Mr Glover is a genius at this sort of thing. During the day we're exploring the local, rural environment and during the lengthening evenings, Mr Glover, Mr Heath, Miss Atkinson and Miss Bates organise all sorts of sporting tournaments and other fantastic activities.

Tonight, I know there's mischief in the air but like Fagin the miser, I'm far too busy counting my pocket money. I keep it hidden in my sock, inside my shoe, in the cupboard under the bed. My mam has given me fifteen bob for the tuck shop for the week and here I am counting it out in the half-light. I've a couple of half-a-crowns, four two-bob pieces and four sixpences, making a grand total of fifteen shillings (75p metric). Thank God nothing's been nicked. I need every penny so I can go to The Famous Army Stores on Eldon Street this Friday and buy my very first football shirt -a red and white Barnsley FC one. They're twice dearer anywhere else and I've also found a clever way of topping-up my savings. Some of the older lads offer me a tanner (six pence) to ask girls to go out with them. It's easy money.

Tonight, everyone's talking about this daring adventure. The proposal is to sneak over to the girls' dormitories after lights-out, just for a dare. I'm uneasy. Usually, I'm up for mischief but I'm not convinced about this one. It's now past midnight and most boys are sat up in bed in the dark, dressed in their pyjamas, either eager to join the expedition or keen to laugh at its failure. We occasionally send a scout out to the toilets to recce the corridors and gather intelligence on whether the teachers' bedroom lights are still on. At 00:25 hrs, it looks all clear. We're ready to go. Then we hear a noise just outside our dormitory door. Is it a member of staff or someone from another dorm trying to spook us?

"Shhh, it's Glover!" whispers someone in the dark and we're under the covers before you can utter the name, "Peg Leg" (The legendary Scout Dyke ghost).

The corridor lights show the silhouette of a big head through the small square of frosted glass in the door. It looks like Mr Glover, alright. We wait nervously. Mr Glover turns the brass door knob stealthily and a crack of corridor light shoots into our dorm. Then very slowly, silently, the light expands as the door is opened wider. There's the sound of giggling and suddenly about ten excited girls burst in. We are all in complete shock and our plans have been well and truly upstaged. One of the older girls, nicknamed Bluey, pulls back my bedclothes and jumps straight into bed alongside me. She's the kind of young woman who sees me as 'cute', like a harmless ornament or little pet dog. I've been sweet on her for months and inside my satchel I've written, "Oliver LOVES Nancy" in order to declare my love but, at the same time, to throw Nosey-Parkers off the scent. I'm nervous but okay with her in my bed because she's so incredibly gorgeous and I'm the type who can hardly speak to a girl without stuttering and blushing... unless it's for money. Most of the other lasses find a partner and do the same, as though it's all been meticulously planned. My heart beats like a blacksmith's hammer but before I can make sense of things, Bluey takes hold of my hand and tugs me out of bed. I bump on the floor like a teddy bear as she whispers loudly to the others,

"Come on, let's take 'em back to ours."

I hesitate but Charlie says, "There's a tanner in it if you go, Ronnie".

Look after my fifteen bob, Charlie" I say. "It's under my pillow" and off I go to my doom – with the ten girls and six lads, footslapping our way through the no-go area to the girls' wing. One of the seven is Glen Snodgrass, the charmer. He broke his leg on the first day of camp, had a pot put on it at Beckett's Hospital and was back at Scout Dyke by tea-time. He's on crutches clicking his way into trouble at the rear of our train. Shockingly, when we get to the girls' side we are ambushed by the wiley Miss Atkinson, in hairnet and dressing gown. Gulp!

"You lot better turn round and go straight back to your own sleeping quarters quickly and prepare your defence for Mr Glover in the morning. You're a disgrace!" she says, screwing up her eyes because she isn't wearing her specs.

When we get back to Dormitory One, our mates offer little comfort.

"You were mad trying that on."

"Glover told us we'd be sent straight back to school to face Hitler, if we strayed into the lasses dorms".

"Phew! Sooner you than me. He's alright, Glover, until he's upset".

"You'll get expelled for this, no doubt!"

"I thought you'd got more oil in your lamp."

"Ronnie Steele'll do owt for a tanner".

I feel sick. Tomorrow morning I face Mr Glover and Mr Heath, then back to school for the cane from Adolph Hopkins, followed by expulsion and finally I'll have to tell my mam and dad. I might as well forget my new Barnsley football shirt and watching Barnsley beat Barrow. My God! What have I done... just for sixpence to go towards a blooming football shirt?

It's daylight outside now and I'm still wide awake, and I'm thinking through the forthcoming trial of the century, over and over again.

Breakfast time for 90 teenagers is just like a funeral wake. When the plates have been cleared we hear Mr Glover's chair scrape and scream as he stands up. He's got his wrestler's face on. Silence.

"At 9 o'clock, those boys who got lost last night and were found wandering in a state of bewilderment in an off-limits area... can leave their packed suitcases in the foyer, ready to return to school. Then they can queue outside the staff quarters where they will be dealt with appropriately. Miss Atkinson and Miss Bates will be dealing with the girls. The rest of you will meet outside the main entrance at 9:30, in your groups, to collect your packed lunches, ready to go on another exciting, exploratory walk." I hear some of the girls sobbing. I look across at Bluey just as she's looking at me. She blows me a surreptitious kiss; I immediately look down at the floor.

Oh, I wish I could turn the clock back. I'm dead scared, but have far too much pride to beg forgiveness. Losing self-respect is worse than facing the music. We're lined up and our suitcases are ready to be loaded into Mr Heath's, Austin Healey. It doesn't dawn on me how he plans to ferry seventeen cases and seventeen students back to school in a small car. Now we have to face Mr Glover's wrath. One by one, we go in and one by one come out, all glum-faced except John Davies and Wyn Brown who refuse to apologise and emerge from the torture chamber looking incredibly cocky. It puts me off them. I'm last in line and Glen Snodgrass is just before me.

"Get in there Snodgrass" says Mr Glover as though he's disgusted, and as Snoddy hobbles through into the Interview Room on his crutches, Mr Glover's seems to have difficulty keeping a straight face. I don't know how Snoddy manages it. He always seems to get away with murder and soon he emerges from the inquisition with a massive smile on his face and no hint of worry about being sent home. Wish I was more like him and Bluey. Then it's my turn. I bear up quite well, full of genuine contrition until Mr Glover says, "And what's your mother and father going to say when they hear about this?" This is too much for me and I feel like rooaring*. Oh, no! It's bad enough getting into trouble without crying like an infant! I only just manage to hold things together by picturing myself in my new football shirt.

Later, all the groups wait outside the front entrance of the centre with their packed lunches. We, the exiled, stand with our suitcases slightly apart from them. Then Mr Glover announces with great ceremony that the teachers, after careful consideration, have decided, against their better judgement, to put the night-time incident down to a foolhardy prank. Therefore, the wayward will NOT be sent home, after all.

A spontaneous, deafening cheer goes up as we return our groups.

Hallelujah! My head is full of cannon-fire and the 1812 Overture. It's feels better than scoring a goal for school. I'm bursting to celebrate: Da da da da da da da da, boom! boom! Da da da da da da da da, boom! boom!

"Now take your suitcases and put them back in the foyer" says Mr Glover, with mock disgust still written on his face.

As we carry our cases towards the main building, Mr Glover bawls out,

"Davies! Brown! Where do you think you're going? You'll need your cases for the hike."

"What?!? Walking with suitcases? That's not right, Sir. What about the others?" says Brown.

"All the others apologised, you two didn't. But if you prefer to explain things to Mr Hopkins... Oh and by the way, you'll both be delighted to hear that I'm part of your group today" he adds. And off they go, lugging their packed cases onto the coach for the short journey to Wharncliffe Crags.

Phew! This has been such a traumatic nine or so hours. Thank God my world has returned to near-normal. I'm not going to be expelled, caned or humiliated and I'm going to be able to buy my Barnsley shirt, after all. I feel a massive weight lifted off my troubled shoulders and such tremendous gratitude to the teachers. I honestly feel I've stared disaster in the face and lived to tell the tale. I'll never do anything like that ever again. Ever! I swear! To me, Mr Glover has become an even greater hero. He's not just saved my life but, far more importantly, he's also rescued my chance of becoming a professional footballer. After all what kind of proud football club takes on delinquents who've been expelled from school?

On their arrival back at the Centre, Davies and Brownie now appear decidedly uncocky. Word goes round that they've both made a grovelling apology and asked permission to go to the final night disco. They crawl onto their respective beds and drop to sleep in a trice with their shoes and all their clothes on. They sleep for two whole hours without even turning over, and miss evening dinner.

However, by seven o'clock they're both alive and kicking by way of the Brain Glover Rehabilitation Scheme and are told they may go to the disco. Unfortunately, I collapse onto my bed just before the disco starts and sleep for eleven and a half hours until breakfast.

Our week at Scout Dyke comes to an end for all of us on the Friday and we return to school just after lunch to be told we're allowed home early. I drop my stuff off at home, get changed and go into Shawland's Football Field and lay on the grass in the sun to consider a wonderful yet traumatic week. As I mull over the incidents of the past five days, I stare up at the changing cloud-shapes. Soon I drift off to sleep for a few minutes, still catching up on what I've missed, and dream about my beautiful Barnsley FC shirt. It's wet and hanging on a makeshift washing line inside Dormitory One. There's something wrong but I don't know what. It makes me feel troubled. When I awake I feel the fifteen bob in my trouser pocket and set off straight to The Famous Army Stores with creepy crawlies in my shirt from the grass. That evening I wear my beautiful new shirt under my jacket and stand behind the goal in the Kop end, at Oakwell. Now, I begin to daydream that Barnsley are a player short and I'm invited to play because I'm the only one in the crowd with a red and white shirt; like in the cartoons when they shout: "Is there a doctor in the house?" But in my imagination I can hear the announcer asking: "Is there a left winger in the house, with a Barnsley shirt?"

Monday morning I get my new shirt from the ironing basket, freshly washed. I hold it up. The white piping round the neck and cuffs has gone pink and the whole thing seems misshapen. I put it on over my school shirt and find it doesn't come down to my belly button but is baggy enough to fit round Desperate Dan.

"I've told you before, you only get cheap rubbish from the Army Stores" says my mam as she drags the twin-tub washer towards the sink area. "You'll listen to me one day".

So my fifteen bob was totally wasted and I missed the disco to boot, but I don't care one jot. Mr Glover handled the situation perfectly and at least I know my future, as a famous international footballer, is not now threatened.

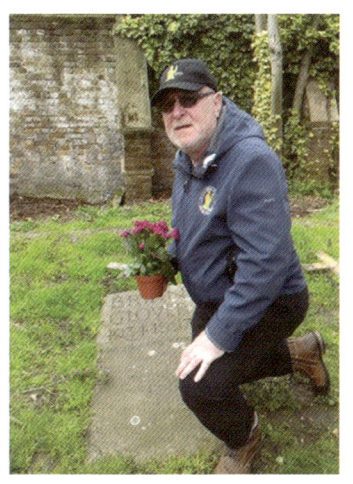

*rooaring is a local slang word meaning crying.

Me putting a pot plant on Brian Glover's grave at Brompton Cemetery, London.

CHAPTER THIRTEEN

THE WINDS OF CHANGE AVOID LONGCAR CENTRAL

The 1960s is a time of inexorable social and political change throughout the world. In our little town, change is embraced in some areas but in others, it's steadfastly opposed. Mr Hopkins doesn't welcome change. He's on the side of tradition which means he'd much rather spoil the rod than spare the child, and he's not prepared to concede a fraction of an inch.

If you ever bumped into Mr Hopkins there's a good chance that you'd feel a degree of sympathy for him. He looks so scruffy, he could easily be confused for someone who's down on his luck. He wears exactly the same shabby suit, frayed shirt and tattered tie that he's worn everyday for the last three years and he always needs a shave. But if you happened to speak to him you'd soon discover he's not a very nice person. His violent temper is frequently out of control, which puts the fear of God in every living thing that crosses his path – teachers, students, parents, the milkman, the postman, pets, birds, anyone. They say even stray dogs scurry out of his way when they see him approaching. He has no friends and doesn't want any. Tyrants don't have friends, they have yes-men and sycophants. On the very rare occasions he's seen in town, those who recognise him, bow their head and walk straight past, pretending not to have seen him, or stop and turn to walk the other way. That's how he prefers it. No kids ever sing Xmas carols at his door and if a child's football happens to accidentally find its way into his garden, it's abandoned to rot.

In 1967 Mr Hopkins is the head teacher of Longcar Central Selective Secondary School of which I am a third year pupil. He's so proud to emphasise 'selective' at the top of the School Report form, as though being part of his school is something to boast about. Indeed, those who happen to visit or walk past the school might be well impressed with the smartness of the school uniform and the hospital-like quietness of the corridors. However, scratch below the surface and you'll discover a surfeit of bullying, unrest and discontent. Many students feel Mr Hopkins runs the school like a borstal, with no trust, freedom or pleasure. In fact a rumour circulates that he once worked as the head of an Approved School but there's no evidence to support this. Mrs Gascoyne, one of our caring teachers, once informed us that there are lots of rules at Longcar but none are written down. "You'll soon pick them up" she says; and we do, but only by breaking them and suffering the backlash. You might discover the hard way, for example, that school uniform is one of Hopkins' top priorities – almost as important as 'unquestioning obedience'. If students have on the wrong colour shirt, for instance, or fail to wear a beret or cap when near school, they're either caned by Hopkins or put into detention. Talking, in the corridor or in lessons, is strictly forbidden except in Games, Woodwork, Metalwork and Domestic Science.

Former students say that before Hopkins arrived it was quite a vibrant school, but soon the thriving Drama Group is terminated; the Parents and Teachers Association is also wound up, and in fact Open Evenings cease to be held. Furthermore, there's no Sports Day, no school choir or orchestra, no cricket or netball or rounders team, no swimming team or swimming gala, no Summer Fair, no Harvest Festival, no Chess Club and no school trips - apart from the annual Scout Dyke Camp visit. Many feel that the general atmosphere at Longcar Central Selective Secondary School has become both stultifying and grim.

Teachers are told to address the head as 'headmaster' or 'Mr Hopkins' but it's said that *nobody* is allowed to know his first name, never mind use it; consequently, 'Adolph' is what some wags secretly settle on. His staff deal with his despotic behaviour in their own way. Some take their cue from him and become his vicious lieutenants, hoping to get their badge polished. Others try their best to improve the school's ethos in spite of him, while at the same time nervously treating professional life as though it's covered in booby-traps.

One afternoon break time, Mr Glover is sat in the Staff Room looking a bit down in the mouth. His friend, Barry Hines, head of PE, walks in.

"Why are you looking so worried, Brian?" says Barry, as he prises the lid off the Nescafe tin with a spoon. "Are you wrestling tonight"?

"Yeah, for sure, I've got a painful engagement with Pedro the Gypsy in Manchester, but that doesn't bother me. It's *this* that's causing me concern" and he tosses Barry a brown envelope.

Barry sucks the air in through his teeth as he notices the handwriting on the envelope is that of Mr Hopkins. "Gulp!" says Barry, teasing. "It must be like getting the Black Spot from Blind Pew." Brian doesn't laugh. He's genuinely sick to his stomach. Then Barry unfolds the white paper and reads it allowed:

"MEMO

Re Boys' Playground Games.

Dear Mr Glover,

Please see me in my office at 4 pm today regarding the above practices.

Regards,

Headmaster."

"What's that all about?" asks Barry as he fills his cup up with boiling water.

"Oh, it's only a craze the lads are going through. They play this game at break time called Pie Crust, which I don't mind, but Hopkins wants it banning. I can see me being lambasted for allowing it when I was on duty, yesterday. You weren't there at the public scolding I got last week? Hopkins went into a paroxysm of rage, literally frothing at the mouth."

"Hang on a minute. Are you're telling me you're more scared of a tongue-lashing from our dapper headmaster than fighting the wild Gypsy?" says Barry, smiling.

"Well, wouldn't you be?"

"Hmmm, now you mention it..."*

By the end of the last lesson that day, Mr Hopkins is in a foul mood. He thinks his staff are being too soft and deliberately undermining him in order to make him look a fool. When he's like this he's been known not to bother caning kids, but to knock them clean off their feet by swiping them across the face with the palm of his hand.

At 3:45 there are two students outside his office: Big Stan Mincher from a third year class has been waiting there for forty minutes. The slightly older Christopher Rawlinson's behind him, and is about to be caned for wearing non regulation, red socks.

Stan Mincher has thick blonde hair. He never displays emotion and usually says very little – a bit like Clint Eastwood in some of his earlier roles. He uses this persona to make his friends laugh but if you are not in tune with his dry humour I imagine it can feel quite disconcerting. When he started at Longcar he was taller and had bigger muscles than the rest of us. Now, three years later, he's grown even more and is built like an American footballer. I've never seen him fight because usually he's no need to. He's just too big. All he has to do is look mean and enemies retreat. Today he's been caught playing Pie Crust by Hopkins himself, even before it's been banned. Hopkins is apoplectic with rage and utters the dreaded words:

"Go to my room boy... and stay there until home time." Except he doesn't say 'room' he says 'rum'

As students quietly file out of school at home time, Hopkins comes to his office door and looks up at big Stan. Like a giant polar bear, Stan looks down on Mr Hopkins. Hopkins realises immediately that Stan's far too big to knock to the floor in a temper tantrum. It would be like trying to push down the walls of the old school air-raid shelters. "Get into my office" he says and waves him through. There's no explanation, no mitigation, no excuses. It's guilty as charged and take your punishment like a man or cry like a big baby. He's not even asked for Stan's name. Hopkins snatches a stick from the cane bin. "Put your hand out, boy." But big Stan keeps his hands by his side. Hopkins scrutinises Stan's face. He's vexed that he sees not a flicker of fear. Stan stares back at Hopkins as though he's playing a game of, *Who Blinks First*. Hopkins tells him again: "Put your damned hand out boy, like a man, I say". The response from Stan is the same. His stare is really scary and it's spooking Hopkins. This has never happened before. We've all witnessed Stan doing this in the playground or in the street and it always looks for a while as if he's going to suddenly snap and tear his opponent's head off, but he never does. There's a long pause but Hopkins blinks first and the stand-off is over. Hopkins has backed down, Stanley Mincher has won. "Go on! Get out of my sight!" shouts Hopkins and don't let me find you outside my office again."

This must be Mr Hopkins' unlucky day because next in line for the cane is Chris Rawlinson. Chris is guilty of wearing red socks because he's heard that's what the Beatles wear. He follows Hopkins into his office which overlooks the internal garden. The late afternoon sun makes the room very hot. Chris has mentally prepared himself for a beating. He sees Hopkins warming up by swishing his cane sideways as though he's decapitating tall daffodils.

"Red socks, indeed. Red socks!" shouts Hopkins, and Chris's not sure whether it's the actual colour or the breaking of the school rule that offends so much. "And what will we get next if wearing red socks goes unpunished? I'll tell you what we'll get: We'll get pink underwear and psychedelic shirts, and chaos and anarchy, no doubt! And before you know it, you'll be turning my school into one of those, those, opium dens!"

Hopkins is really working himself up into a frenzy. Chris imagines scores of hippies walking round the internal school garden in pink underwear, smoking marijuana and giggling. He has to bite his lip to stop himself from smirking.

"Take your trousers and underpants down, boy" he tells Chris.

Chris's eyes widen. Did he hear that right? Did Hopkins actually say, take your trousers and underpants down? In a state of shock Chris blurts out incredulously: "Tha what?!"

"Don't 'thee and tha' me, boy! Take your trousers and underpants down and bend over!" screams Hopkins, as he swishes the cane, excitedly.

"Take my trousers and underpants down?!?" This is too much for Chris. The very thought makes him nauseous. He automatically snatches the cane out of the grasp of Hopkins and walks straight to the exit door.

"Come back here, boy, now!" shouts Hopkins, but Chris is already stepping into the secretary's office and pushing past Mr Glover, mumbling, "If I do come back in here again, I'll come back with my father."

The next day, Hopkins doesn't mention the incident and it's never referred to again.**

Brian Glover is limping badly after his fight with Pedro the Gypsy. He tells his colleagues that Hopkins had to cancel the arranged meeting because he says he had a migraine, but Brian knows better.

Barry Hines wonders how he can use the dictatorial behaviour of Hopkins in a new book he's writing about a boy and a kestrel.***

The winds of change are definitely blowing throughout all four corners of the earth. They're just late to arrive at Longcar Central School.

* Brian Glover often admitted that he was far more fearful of Hopkins than he was of Pedro the Gypsy wrestler.

** As recounted by Chris Rawlinson himself.

*** In 1993 Barry Hines tells me that Mr Grice, in Kes, was partly based on Mr Hopkins.

Chris Rawlinson

Garry Blake

Stan Mincher

CHAPTER FOURTEEN

THE SHEER BRILLIANCE OF BRIAN GLOVER

It's April 1968 and we are part-way through a year which would later be described by many as the most tumultuous in history. Film footage of the My Lai Massacre inflicted by US forces in Vietnam is seen by millions. Martin Luther King is assassinated and there's suspicion the US government has had a hand in it. Social revolution is about to kick-off in France and Simon and Garfunkel dominate the charts with Mrs Robinson. Meanwhile at Longcar Central School...

We're in the run-up to Easter. The novel, Kestrel for a Knave, written by our PE teacher, Barry Hines, has already been published eight weeks previously but Brian Glover has no idea that he will be chosen to play Mr Sugden in the film, Kes.

I've always enjoyed History lessons and Mr Glover is the type of inspirational figure that I would gladly walk barefoot over broken glass to please. I work extremely hard to make sure I'm always at, or near, the top of the class in History, though I really can't be bothered in most other subjects. I'm expecting today to be just another day but we are in for a pleasant surprise.

We file into Mr Glover's classroom. Something's different. The display boards at the back of the room are filled with large, homemade booklets, not much smaller than a desktop, constructed from brightly coloured paper. Also, placed upon the cupboard tops, immediately below the booklets, are artefacts and models relating to them. I see sports' medals, war medals, birth certificates, framed photos, cardboard models etc. We're all intrigued because apart from the rare educational posters, the walls of Longcar Central School are usually as bare as that of a prison cell. Mr Glover, in white shirt, dark tie and fawn sports jacket, stands near the far windows overlooking the playground and says nothing. I recognise the authors of these extraordinary pieces of work. They are of 14 to 15 year old pupils from the Fourth Year... the year above us.

Mr Glover waves his hand towards the display like a polite person offering you priority through the doorway. We all gather at the back wall to see what's on offer.

I'm immediately impressed by the lettering and decorations on the front of the booklets. They're bold, colourful, large, different and creative. Normally, everything is incredibly uniform at Longcar, from the regulation school clothes to the pencil-margin on every page and the date to be written before every new piece of work. None of us has ever seen students' work presented in this flamboyant way before. The titles are even more impressive:

"WHEN GEORGE ORWELL CAME TO BARNSLEY", "THE STORY OF CANNON HALL", "MY GRANDDAD'S PART IN THE FIRST WORLD WAR", "THE HISTORY OF ST MARY'S CHURCH", "THE LIFE OF DOROTHY HYMAN", "MY FAMILY HISTORY", THE HISTORY OF BARNSLEY FOOTBALL CLUB", "THE STORY OF MONK BRETTON PRIORY", "MY MOTHER LIVED ON THE BAREBONES", "BOXING".

Wow! I realise these students have been given the freedom and responsibility to choose not only what they want to study but also how they study it. I'm immediately hooked. I look to snatch the 'Barebones' booklet because that's the famous area where my mam was raised, but it's whisked away before I can unhook it. So, as a keen Barnsley fan I grab the Barnsley FC history, even though I would have been delighted with any of the titles.

Me and Alan sit at our desk and two others peek over our shoulders. We open up the booklet and skim-read the whole thing, cover-to-cover. I'm astonished. This reads much better than any 'real' book and it's written by someone roughly my age who I actually know! Suddenly I notice there's noise in the classroom. This is unusual because all talking is prohibited in academic subjects and in the school corridors... often with good reason. It inhibits learning, we are often reminded. But this noise is not idle chatter; it's of an intellectual nature, relating to the subject matter at hand. When we reach the end of the booklet our group returns back to the beginning and starts studying each page in forensic detail.

We see sketches, photos, photos of old photos, question-and-answer interviews, surveys, copies of letters sent as requests, short texts and longer ones written with care, pride and precision. We discover that Barnsley Football Club was founded by a vicar, Reverend Tiverton Preedy, at St Peter's Church on Doncaster Road and was originally named Barnsley St Peter's. I know this church because I pass it regularly and it's not that far from where I live. There's a photo of Barnsley in stripes! and one of Reverend Preedy himself. Suddenly, that blasted, inconsiderate school bell, signalling the end of the lesson, interferes with our concentration.

"Ey up! That's a short lesson", I say, closing the booklet and picking up my satchel.

"Don't think so, it just seemed it", says Alan checking his watch.

On my way out I get that warm feeling you experience when leaving the cinema after a classic film.

By the number of girls around Mr Glover, thanking him for the lesson, I realise I'm not the only one who's been completely immersed in real, enjoyable learning. Mr Glover is perhaps even more popular with the female students as he is with the lads but this is the first time I've witnessed students thanking a teacher for delivering any lesson... and the significant thing is, Mr Glover has hardly said a word during the whole half-hour.

Then I hear for the first time, the shouting and screaming of the Fourth Year girls playing netball on the Girls' Playground just outside Mr Glover's window. They must have been calling and whooping, amidst blasts of Miss Bates's whistle, throughout our lesson and I noticed nothing.

As we walk down the corridor to Miss Gould's Geography Room with the gardened, internal quadrangle on our left, and the late morning sun streaming through the glass, I can't get this lesson out of my mind. It occupies my thoughts for the rest of the day and for weeks afterwards, completely dominating my imagination. I want to be part of this experiment. I would dearly love to decide what I want to discover and how I research and present it. I imagine the books I would have to consult, the libraries I would visit, the letters I would have to send, the questionnaires I would construct, the people I would interview. My first chosen topics could be:

THE HISTORY OF THE VIETNAM WAR UP TO 1968

by Ronnie Steele.

Or: TOMMY TAYLOR AND MARK JONES – the Busby Babes from Barnsley.

By Ronnie Steele

Or: Sir Winston Churchill

By Ronnie Steele.

Or maybe even: BODICEA, QUEEN OF THE ICENI TRIBE

By Ronnie Steele.

My mate goes much further than me. He actually spends his entire Easter holiday finding out about his hero, Admiral Lord Nelson and presenting his findings in a book. He loves the experience. Now that is impressive. So it seems I'm not the only student blown away by this alternative view of teaching and learning.

Unfortunately, Longcar Central School is closing in just a few weeks time because of the advent of the comprehensive system to be introduced two years hence. The boys are destined for Holgate Grammar School, the girls for Barnsley Girls High School and Mr Glover is transferring to the English department at Racecommon Road Secondary Modern School. I feel robbed. It's not fair.

Holgate has a reputation for being literally one of the finest schools in the country but it's not that different to Longcar. The head, Mr Smith, presides over a much kinder regime but although there are one or two outstanding teachers, they are, on average, no better than our Longcar teachers. The significant thing is, the basic teaching methods of both schools are almost identical. The teachers talk, explain, demonstrate and the students passively digest what they are fed, ready to regurgitate it on the day of the test. And they do have a good excuse... they must teach to the tests to obtain the prestigious 'O' Level results.

Years later I talk to other successful Longcar alumni who appreciate Brian Glover's forward thinking and it does cross my mind that Mr Glover must have stuck his neck out experimenting with these modern teaching techniques. Perhaps Mr Hopkins and some others might have seen these new-fangled ideas as a threat to their tyrannical control? Having young people asking questions that you perhaps don't know the answers to, can feel threatening.

I will always believe Mr Glover's revolutionary methods are far superior to the traditional. Becoming an independent learner, devising questions, thinking for oneself, learning for pleasure, gaining self-belief, knowledge and skills, should, in my view, be the goals of every educational establishment, in every part of the world, at any time. When it does occur you see human beings grow mentally and emotionally; the progress is obvious and it feels good, even if it can't be measured. However, when it doesn't happen, I believe a golden opportunity is lost.

The big question is this: Do those who control our children's education really want to be turning out independent, confident, accomplished learners, or is this seen as a threat to the status quo?

Mr Glover spent years taking risks by pushing at the boundaries and later, as a teacher myself, so did I.

CHAPTER FIFTEEN

BARRY HINES AND THE PUDDING BALL - SUMMER 1968

First day back after the Spring Bank Half-Term holiday, 1968, and we're on the final lap before our school, Longcar Central, is closed for good. Personally I'll not be shedding any tears but at the same time I'm not really aware of how much I'm going to miss Mr Hines, Mr Glover and a few other dedicated teachers.

Gordon Green hasn't done PE for a number of weeks. He hates sport so he brings a note from his mam with a different excuse every time. Mr Hines is ok with this especially as Greenie brings a big bag of sweets and always offers him one as he presents the note. Today, Mr Hines takes us outside in the sunshine and sits us on the sloping grass bank between the school and the boys' playground. There are two, pristine-looking, leather bags sat on the low wall at the edge of the playground. Greenie isn't in his PE gear again.

"Green! Unfit again lad? Have you brought a note?" says Mr Hines, with half a smile. He puts his hand inside one of the leather bags and takes out a brand new cricket bat. I wonder for a second whether Mr Hines is going to chase him round the playground with it and I smile because I know Mr Hines wouldn't harm a wasp even if it stung him.

"No, Sir. Forgotten it, Sir."

"Have you got any sweets?" asks Mr Hines.

"Yes, Sir".

"That'll do then," and Mr Hines takes a sweet, pops it in his mouth and carries on with the lesson, as we all laugh.

"It's cricket twice a week for you boys this half term."

"Yes!" we all chorus, excitedly.

Ged has a worry and interrupts Mr Hines in full flow. "We've been at Longcar for three years and we've never been allowed to play cricket because we're surrounded by windows, Sir. In fact I don't think anyone's played cricket here for decades."

"I think you might find that's not going to be a problem, Wilcock" replies Mr Hines.

This must mean we're playing with a tennis ball so we're all feeling fed-up because there's little fun playing cricket with a 'softie'. That's bairns' cricket.

Mr Hines puts his hand in his hip pocket and pulls out a wallet and shows us about half a dozen one pound notes. Everyone's eyes light up. Six pounds is not far off a council worker's weekly wage.

"If anyone can hit this cricket ball and reach the dining room windows, I'll give him a new one pound note" he says. "However, I have to tell you all, this is not your regular, MCC, cricket ball. It's a little bit softer and a lot, lot heavier. It's called a pudding ball." Then he throws it really hard towards the tarmac near his toes and the pudding ball only just bounces up above Mr Hines's knees. He then tosses the ball to Ian Ellis for him to feel it and pass it round while he fetches an identical ball from the bag.

Alan Newsam, Ged and Bri Stanyon are the first three in the queue ready to smash a window and collect their reward. These three 14 year olds are all as powerful as adults. Al is handed the same bat that Mr Hines took out of the bag and he notices not only that it's unused, but it also has the 'ancient' cricketing name, Len Hutton, inscribed on it.

"Blimey! Len Hutton was my dad's hero" chuckles Al Newsam, with heavy irony, as he takes the stance with the bat. "Did you get these out of a museum, Sir?" Mr Hines bowls him a half-pace delivery and Al takes an elegant skip towards the bowler and slogs the ball skywards with all his might. I look up into the sun to track its trajectory but just after contact, the pudding ball changes shape, becoming almost disc-like, spins and swerves and bounces tamely only twenty yards away. It reminds me of that circus trick when a cannonball is fired, only for it to just drop out of the end of the barrel. Anti climax, or what? Everyone on the grassy bank is rolling around, in stitches.

"It's like batting away a football", says Al, justifying his unspectacular effort. The next two batsmen also fail miserably so Mr Hines's point is made and he saves a few pounds.

We're on half-classes for PE now so two teams of seven players are picked. It's a seven-overs game and every fielder must bowl one over. Then Mr Hines gets a real cricket scoring book and pencil from the bag and says,

"Riddiough. Show Green how to score and he might give you a sweet."

Dave Riddiough has spent every summer since he was six, following Yorkshire cricket at Headingley and Scarborough, filling in his own proper scoring book. I haven't a clue how Mr Hines knows this. Is he a mind reader?

Actually bringing us this score book turns out to be a masterstroke. It's a professional one, the real McCoy and Mr Hines is magically transforming Longcar Central School playground into The Lords Cricket Ground. Our team, India, are batting first so we all get properly padded-up and gloved-up and sit on the grass banking waiting our turn. Gordon Green is sat with us, genuinely keen to follow Dave Riddiough as he demonstrates the art of scoring.

Ged and I have spent hours and hours watching Test cricket on TV and mimicking the wonderful commentary skills of Richie Benaud and Brian Johnson. This is the perfect stage for our magnificent (we think) double-act. I do the Ozzie accent of Benaud and Ged speaks like the upper class, 'Johnners'. Barry Hines is behind the stumps at the bowlers end, umpiring and within earshot. Wonder if we can make him smile?

Ged goes first.

BRIAN JOHNSON: Welcome BBC One viewers to a day of wonderful international Test cricket in these glorious conditions here at the Lords Cricket Ground, Barnsley.

(Mr Hines hears Ged perfectly but is ignoring him and trying to keep a straight face. Then as Ian Douglas is caught at mid-on for only 2 runs, it's my turn to play Richie Benaud and make him laugh.)

RICHIE BENAUD: And he's gone! He's out! Douglas is caught at mid-on, only 98 runs short of his century.

(Mr Hines covers his mouth with his right hand to hide his mirth, we think. Now it's back to Ged -aka Brian Johnson).

BRIAN JOHNSON: As bowler David Thwaites starts his run up, Winker Watson is fielding at leg slip for Pakistan, with his legs wide open, waiting for a tickle.

(Mr Hines rolls his eyes and shakes his head but he has broken into a smile. Success! Yes!)

This first Test Match is very close but we just squeak it. Towards the end of the game Mr Hines stops play to have a word with me. My desire to win leads me to urge a couple of our India players not to throw their wicket away cheaply. Mr Hines sees this as unsporting and intimidating.

"Don't shout at your own players, Steele, as though they're not trying. You'll just make them shrink into their shell" he says. But his voice has no edge to it. He's not threatening, he's patiently educating and I'm listening.

That summer, India and Pakistan play sixteen Test matches on our Lord's Playground and not one window is ever in danger of being smashed. The competition is fierce; the skill development is phenomenal and the pleasure we all get is off the scale. Every game is decided in the last over and sometimes with the last ball. This eight-week period is the greatest of my life. The sun shines, it seems, every day from dawn 'til dusk and it never rains. Faced with the problem of not having a sports field Mr Hines shows his ability to problem-solve by introducing the revolutionary pudding ball. Furthermore, the student who's always skiving PE is now a keen scorer and doesn't thereafter miss a lesson or bring a note- only a bag of sweets to bribe the teacher. This sends a message directly to my consciousness that for every problem there's a solution. Now, looking back I can't for the life of me think of a more important attitude that educators can instil.

At the end of July, Longcar Central closes. That August the very young Ken Loach and Tony Garnett come to Barnsley with a technical crew to shoot the film, Kes. Some of the older Longcar students are auditioned and selected for parts in the iconic movie. The boys from our school-year are transferred to Holgate Grammar School. We've already been on a visit to see their fabulous facilities: lots of football pitches; a hockey pitch; long jump, high jump and discus throwing areas; a purpose-built gym; several cricket pitches including a beautiful, grass, cricket square; and luxury coaches to take us to play other grammar schools throughout South Yorkshire for a Saturday morning football league. However, Holgate doesn't have the magical, Longcar Central, all-weather pitch, which philistines might describe as merely a playground. And despite some outstanding teachers and a beautifully manicured grass wicket, cricket at our new school is never the same.

Incidentally, the closure of Longcar Central School starts a deep passion for cricket-scoring for one student but also heralds the end of 'promising' careers, for two comic commentators.

What I wouldn't do to find that cricket scoring book from our summer of perfect contentment?

Ged Wilcock

CHAPTER SIXTEEN

THE PEAKS AND TROUGHS OF PLAYING FOR BARNSLEY BOYS – 1968/9

Being picked to play football for the Barnsley Schools Under 15s team, is regarded as a huge honour and is enormously prestigious for the school the player attends. Household names like Tommy Taylor, Dickie Bird, Alan Woodward, Alan Hill, Eric Winstanley, Pat Howard, Stuart Barraclough, Frank Casper, Jimmy Greenoff, Brian Greenoff, Steve Daley, Phil Chambers et al, all started their rise to fame by playing for the town team. It's even rumoured that the fortunes of the town's schoolboy team is so valued by the Civic Fathers, those teachers involved with the Under 15s are fast-tracked for a headship, if they're ambitious enough.

In September 1964 I am a 10 year old dreamer and the dream is always the same. I'm dribbling down the left wing of the Oakwell pitch, in front of a cheering crowd, beating the fullback then firing the ball into the roof of the net at the kop end.

My dad does his best to keep my feet on the ground by telling me that if I really want to be a professional footballer I've several hurdles to jump. First, I must prove I'm good enough for the Barnsley Under 11s side, and more importantly, I then have to get selected for the Under 15s, when I'm old enough. The only thing is, there are four players better than me in our junior school side so I don't even get sent for trials. I'm really disappointed but I say to my dad,

"Dad, I bet you two bob I play for Barnsley Boys Under 15s in four years time."

"Have you heard what our Ronnie's saying, Mary? I'm going to write that down and put it in t'drawer" says my dad to my mother. The piece of paper, with the bet written on it, is then placed at the back of the sideboard drawer and completely forgotten.

A couple of weeks later I experience the greatest 'high' of my life so far, when I play for Agnes Road Under 11s against Holyrood on Shaw Lane and score four goals. Nothing matches that feeling of putting the ball in the net in a proper game. It's truly mind-blowing, like a musical climax exploding in my head, and for a few minutes I feel like I can succeed at anything.

The next four years are filled with intense football-related activity. My commitment to the game develops from an interest, into a passion, and finally, an obsession. It seems that wherever I go I take a football with me. I play morning, afternoon and night and when I'm not playing I'm usually off with Rob Rookledge or Mark Ashworth to watch some team play. We observe all the Barnsley teams playing at Oakwell – First Team, Reserves, Intermediates (Young professionals), Barnsley School Boys etc. I regularly follow lads of my own age like Phil Chambers, Dougie O'Connor and Brian Greenoff, to see what I can pick up from them. There's also this lad called Brian Mills who plays for Holgate Grammar School who does very clever tricks on a football field that nobody else does, so I watch him closely and copy him. All this sparks a great thirst for knowledge. Everything I read is to do with football and the lives of footballers. I scour the Daily Mirror for sports stories and read every issue of the Sheffield Star and Green 'Un. The very first book I ever volunteer to read is called The W M Formation, which explains the different positions on a football field. I'm soon devouring every publication I can find on the history of football and the biographies of the greats. My knowledge of geography, history and maths is greatly enhanced and my skills in reading and comprehension become developed to a high degree. I'm that interested in the subject matter, every fact I learn attaches itself to my memory like a sticky-bud to a sweater. Moreover, as an eleven year old, I start travelling the country watching Barnsley and sometimes visiting Bramall Lane, Hillsborough or Elland Road with my young mates to watch top First Division fixtures. If I can't afford to pay to watch Barnsley play away I sometimes hitchhike to the away grounds without informing my parents.

By the time I'm twelve, along with Melv Henighan and Alan Newsam, I'm playing football for the year above my age group at Longcar Central School and I'm scoring lots of goals. Brian Glover and Barry Hines are our teachers and I begin to sense that, perhaps, something special is happening. When we play Edward Sheerien away, I knock two early goals past their keeper, Dennis Low, inside the first ten minutes. Barry Hines is late to arrive so he misses my goals but he does see Dennis make a super save from me, from just underneath the crossbar.

The following week I score two early goals against Racecommon Road, who have Brian Greenoff and Arnie Sidebottom in their team. Incidentally, Greenoff forgets his boots that day and has to play in sneakers, but he's so talented he runs the show from midfield. Mr Glover is talking to my dad on the touchline about how brilliant Brian Greenoff is, then he turns to my dad and says.

"Mr Hines is always talking about your Ronnie in the staffroom, you know. He says he plays just like Alan Ball."

"Aye" my dad replies, "and our Ronnie's got a temper like him, an' all."

Wow! Mr Glover's comment doesn't half make a big impression on me. Barry Hines does think I can play, after all! And I suddenly realise that Mr Hines will be exactly the same with other good players, like Trevor Phillips, Geoff English and Mick Padgett. I've heard him many times, waxing lyrical over their footballing skills but I bet he never tells them how good they are to their faces. Maybe he thinks it will go to their heads. Well, I'm certainly not going to let that happen to me.

Mr Hines and Mr Glover send me for the Barnsley Boys' trials at Raley School in September '67 even though I'm still only in my third year at Longcar Central. This is a huge confidence booster but I'm soon brought down to earth when I'm rejected for the squad. My big problem is, I'm just too small.

I attempt all sorts of crazy things to put weight on. I try to over-eat but it just makes me sick. My mother's friend recommends I try raw eggs mixed with sherry but it's like having to take the worst medicine imaginable. I even try weight training down at the Junction to build up some muscle. But the real problem is, I'm a very poor eater. Whereas some folk build up an appetite when doing physical work, the exact opposite happens to me. So I have to endure the predictions that I'll never get picked for Barnsley Under 15s Schoolboys unless I clap weight on... and fast!

However, I still have a fantastic season playing for Longcar Central Under 15s even though I'm only thirteen. For part of the season I play centre forward and become the leading scorer. In one match I'm marked by the current Barnsley Boys centre half, a mountain of a lad called O'Brien, who plays for St Michaels. It seems I don't come much above his waist; nevertheless, I score four goals in one game against them and dribble rings round him

By September 1968 we move from Longcar Central to Holgate Grammar School. This is the moment I've been looking forward to for the last four years. If I can manage to get selected for Barnsley Under 15s, there's a chance I'll be offered a contract with a professional football club. I'm so hungry for success, and all my burning ambition emanates from deep within my being.

Mr Bostwick, the PE teacher at Raley School, and a Barnsley Boys selector, lets it slip that Barry Hines has been raving to him about me as a player and as a consequence he's says he's going to keep a special eye on me. After a series of trials, about twenty boys are selected and my name appears on the list. Hallelujah!

A few days later, our PE teacher at Holgate comes to our form room just before registration. Mr Goodman is an overweight, chain-smoking, German-born, sports fanatic. I love him.

"I vant to see Steele" he says, out of breath from climbing a few steps. "You vill be playing left ving for ze town team against Rotherham, tomorrow. You must bring..."

Mr Goodman's voice begins to fade and all can hear are the fireworks exploding in my head. I've done it! I've only gone and done it! Four years of dreaming and striving and someone has noticed me as a player with promise. Show me a solid brick wall and I'll run straight through it if it means I'll star for the town's schoolboy team.

When I get home my dad is napping on the settee after a shift at the pit.

"Dad! Dad! Wake up! I've been picked for Barnsley Boys against Rotherham tomorrow!" I shout.

My dad's wide awake in a flash. He gets to his feet, goes to the sideboard cupboard and from the drawer he gets out the four year old piece of paper with the bet written on it.

He reads it out aloud to me and my mam.

"Our Ron bets me two-bob that he'll play for Barnsley Schools' Under 15s in 1968.

Signed, Dad.

21st September 1964."

"What do you think to that then, Mary. Aren't you proud of him?" says my dad as he hands me a two-bob piece.

My mam can't speak she's so overcome.

The euphoria doesn't last long. We lose our first two games and I'm dropped. It's a bitter blow but I'm extremely determined to reclaim my spot in the side. My sister's boyfriend starts poking fun and my mam tells me to pack the whole thing in, but there's no chance of that ever happening. I start to feel a bit discouraged but the changes that are made to the side are making no difference to the team's fortunes – we're still getting beaten. Then one morning at registration time, Mr Goodman comes to our form room again.

"I vant to see Steele" he says, looking up and squinting as though the sun is shining in his eyes. "You have been selected as ze number 10 for ze town team to play York Boys at Boozam Crescent, tomorrow. Zis is not a friendly. It's ze first round of ze English Shield. Zis is your chance to shine. Make sure you don't fluff your lines."

"Fluff my lines? There's no chance of that, Mr Goodman" I reply, and I don't. That Wednesday evening we play under the floodlights in York and win 4 – 1 and I have the game of my life.

From then on, my best mate, Ged Wilcock, sees a great opportunity to pull my leg by turning up at the form room door every morning and shouting,

"I vant to see Steele." It's a brilliant impersonation and it creases everyone in our class until one day, unbeknown to Ged, Mr Goodman is actually standing behind him, watching and listening. We're all trying to alert Ged before he gets into too much trouble. However, to Mr Goodman's credit, he just shakes his head and rolls his eyes and simply proceeds to give me the forthcoming match details.

From then on the Barnsley Boys' team becomes unbeatable. We make great progress in the English and Yorkshire Shield competitions and I'm banging in goals right left and centre. Our brilliant coach, Maurice Firth, books us in at Scout Dyke for a week of ideas and instruction from Barnsley first team coach, Norman Rimmington and Barnsley's twin centre backs, Eric Winstanley and Pat Howard. The feeling of confidence and euphoria has returned to me and the team. We feel certain we're going places. On the Thursday evening at Scout Dyke we all watch Top of the Pops on TV and as Mary Hopkins sings her Number One hit, we all join in and we realise this is our perfect theme song.

"Those were the days my friend

We thought they'd never end

We'd sing and dance forever and a day

We'd live a life we choose

We'd fight and never lose

Those were the days

Oh yes those were the days"

From that time onwards we sing our theme song after every victory and our results get better and better. We're successful in every competitive match and lose only one game, away to Manchester Boys, on Maine Road, in a friendly. We don't even field our best team that day because our captain and star player, Dougie O'Connor, is ill, so our confidence is not dented.

By April 1969 we're on the crest of a wave. Eight of our team are chosen to represent Yorkshire Boys and Phil Chambers, our left back, receives the greatest accolade possible when he's selected for England Schoolboys. I'm told by my PE teacher, Mr Goodman, that I've not been picked for Yorkshire because of my size. I can live with that.

In the final of the Yorkshire Shield we are to play Rotherham in a two-legged affair but that is a non event compared to our next English Shield fixture. Having beaten Kirkby (Merseyside) in the quarter-final, containing a certain Phil Thompson at inside left, we are drawn in the semi to play Liverpool School Boys at Oakwell. In the run up to the fixture there's a massive amount of media coverage, especially in the Sheffield Green 'Un. In every shop window and on every notice board there are adverts for the game. Then disaster strikes.

It starts with a tickly cough that at first doesn't worry me. Next day, the cough turns nasty and my head and muscles ache so much I'm sent home from school. The doctor is sent for and by now I'm very ill. Influenza and bronchitis are diagnosed and I'm put on antibiotics. I'm struggling to eat but I make sure my mam gives me a regular fix of the eggs and sherry mixture. My condition deteriorates further and two days before the match, one of the selectors, Mr Eagle, comes to our door to assess my condition. It's clear there's little chance of recovery in time for the big match. I'm so ill I can't even manage to go across the yard to the outside loo, never mind run around a football pitch for a full game. I have to use a potty as a toilet.

On the day of the game I try my best to get up and walk but I can't even stand for more than a few seconds. At five o'clock, the Sheffield Star newspaper comes through our letter box and on the back page I see a short article with the following headline:

"BARNSLEY SCHOOLS FLU BLOW"

So now it's official and in print - I'm missing the most important game of my life. However, I'm not too worried about the outcome. We're still certain to win because we have some outstanding reserves: Billy Cherryholme and John Land have already been snapped up by First Division, Huddersfield Town. There's also big Roy Cole who's been promised a contract by Barnsley FC, and there's Alan Newsam from Holgate and Robert Mooney from Penistone Grammar. Anyway, even if we don't win we'll at least get a draw and I should then be fit for the replay at Anfield. The selectors decide to pick Robert Mooney as my replacement.

My dad sets off for Oakwell and I have to endure the longest two hours of my life while I wait for him to return. At last I hear his footsteps on the pavement outside and see him pressing down the door handle. I sit up from my sick bed and smile but he's not smiling back.

"We lost 3 – 1" he says, and I just can't believe it. My dad sometimes kids me on so I ask him straight out.

"Are you having me on, Dad?" And I'm really expecting him to burst out laughing and tell me the truth.

"No. Most of your mates were heartbroken when the final whistle was blown. We were beaten fair and square by a set of very big lads" he says as he fumbles inside his coat pocket for the match programme. Opening it up I see he's scribbled down the attendance of 7,000 plus, which was announced over the tannoy. This means that over 7,000 spectators turned up for a schoolboy match! Incredible! My dad's also underlined the names of two Liverpool players who were outstanding. I read their names out aloud:

"John Gidman and Ronnie Goodlass."

"Mark my words" my dad says, "These two will make the whole world sit up and listen one day. They're that good. And Ronnie Goodlass has only got one hand but he can make a football talk."

The Chronicle report on the match says that the Liverpool team looked for all the world like they had stepped out from The Land of the Giants.

This defeat is another bitter blow and my illness takes its toll, leaving me very weak. However, I do manage to play in the final of the Yorkshire Shield against Rotherham and we finish up thrashing them, to be crowned the finest team in the county. We might have failed to win the English Shield but becoming the champions of Yorkshire is a very satisfying consolation.

AFTERWORD

Of the two outstanding Liverpool players that night, Ronnie Goodlass, the lad who lost his hand in an accident, has a successful career at Everton and then in Europe and John Gidman plays for Manchester United and is capped for England. Of the Barnsley team, Phil Chambers finishes up captaining Barnsley Football Club for many years.

Playing for Barnsley School Boys was a dream come true for me and the journey to get there was tough but incredibly thrilling. Nowadays, I am able to relive the peaks and troughs of that wonderful season, simply by pressing a button on my computer and hearing Mary Hopkins sing her powerful ballad of nostalgia:

"Those were the days my friend

We thought they'd never end

We'd sing and dance forever and a day

We'd live a life we choose

We'd fight and never lose

Those were the days

Oh yes those were the days"

Barnsley Boys Under 16s

CHAPTER SEVENTEEN

MY VERY BRIEF CAREER AS A COAL MINER

We're in the middle of a bitterly cold spell during the winter of 1984/'85 and my father's been on strike for over ten months.

My mam is working as a part-time cleaner for the council, so by making certain financial cut-backs, and receiving a modest amount of financial support from me, my parents are able to just scrape by. My dad says he's too old for the picket line at 57, and besides, he did his picketing in 1972 when he and his collier-mates spent a week or so in East Anglia, closing down the power stations and the docks.

Last November I bought my mam and dad a tonne of coal to see them through the winter but by early January their stocks are already running low.

Today is particularly cold but at least it's dry and sunny. I set off walking to my mother-in-law's, who lives in Kingstone, by taking a short-cut through the Grammar School fields. It leads to a path at the side of the Fire Station on Broadway. In the distance, just behind the Station, I spot a man on his own, digging on the spare ground. I can see only his head and body but my curiosity is aroused, so I make a beeline for him. Alongside the three-feet deep circular hole he's standing in, is a rusty barrow with a woollen sweater draped over the handles and a pile of brown hessian sacks on the ground.

"What you up to, Mister? Digging for gold? I joke, smiling.

"As good as" replies the man, talking whilst holding a cigarette between his lips. "It's worth as much as gold to me. This'll keep grandbairns warm 'til spring arrives." Then he lifts his spade out of the hole to reveal a heap of shiny black coal. It's his first spadeful and my eyes are saucers.

"Aren't you Fred Steele's son, the teacher?" he asks.

"Yeah, yeah", I say, "and I recognise you, now. You're Mr Renshaw from Gilroyd, aren't you?"

"I am indeed. Here, just hold this sack a minute." And as I open the top of the bag he lets his coal slide into the bottom of it.

When the sack is full I say, "You'll have to excuse me Mr Renshaw because I'm going to fetch my dad and a couple of barrows."

"Tha does reight lad" he answers "but keep this under thi hat or it'll soon be swarming wi folk up here. We don't want coppers to get wise to it, do we?"

I head off at a trot, down the Garden Walks, between the allotments and Shaw Lane Cricket Club, to Harvey Street where my mam and dad live. My dad is excited when I tell him and agrees to meet me back at the new Broadway coal seam, as soon as possible. About twenty minutes later we meet up. I'm wearing my dad's old NCB donkey jacket and wellies with steel toe caps. However, by now, there's more than a dozen folk digging, and looking round, we see twenty to thirty exploratory holes - the majority of which have been abandoned because they drew a blank. I get my spade and dad's pick from the barrow, ready to start.

"Whoa back a minute, son. Let me work out how the seam lies then we'll not waste time" says my dad as he walks round the area like a pro golfer on the putting green. He checks which holes have reached the coal seam and how deep they had to dig. He also has to work out which way the seam is flowing because this will also determine where we dig.

"Look here. See that pattern of successful digs?" he asks, rhetorically. "It hints that the seam is going diagonally from one corner of the field to the other. Now notice at this end of the field, the coal kisses the surface, whereas at the far side, the holes have to be dug deeper to locate the coal."

"And?" I say.

"And so if we dig roundabout this spot, we have a pretty good chance of success straight away" and he lifts up his pick and strikes at the ground, to mark the spot.

My turn first. Half a dozen strikes with the pick and I'm convinced I've qualified as a bona fide coal miner. My dad sits on his haunches, smoking a fag, waiting for his turn. After ten minutes I'm shattered. My biceps are aching and little blisters emerge on my soft teacher's hands. I climb out of the small hole, and the damp clay sticks to my wellies, making them feel as heavy as deep-sea divers' boots. My dad takes over and after ten minutes he's standing in a three-feet deep fox-hole but there's no sign of any fuel. Now it's my shift again. Off comes my donkey jacket and beanie hat but as the hole gets deeper there's still no black gold - only soil, squidgy clay and heaps of stones.

"I'm not impressed with your surveying skills, dad. Aren't we digging in the wrong place, here?" and I feel water on the wooden shaft of the pick that's weeping from the burst blisters on both my hands.

"Oh, ye of little faith" says my dad and at that very moment I look down and do see something jet-black under my feet.

"Hang on a minute... hang on! What's this? what is this?" I say, using the spade as a scraper. "I may be wrong but I've got a feeling we might have struck gold here, father. Play it cool, play it cool."

But Dad can't play it cool. "Oh, you beauty! You absolute beauty!" he shouts, when he spots the black shiny floor at the bottom of the hole, under my boots. It just looks like I'm stood on a sheet of black glass about the diameter of a dustbin lid. As a kid, I often shovelled a coal delivery into our shed, for pocket money, but I've never actually *dug* coal from the ground before and the experience this day is unforgettable. I drive the blade of my spade downwards and find that coal is surprisingly brittle. The metal blade cuts into it, almost as easy as cutting into sand. The coal shatters into a thousand lego-size pieces, all angular, ready to be scooped up and slid into a sack. I can see now where the term 'black diamonds' comes from. My muscles no longer ache and I feel not the slightest pain from my blisters. Fatigue has turned into giddiness.

"Hi ho, hi ho, it's off to work we go

With a shovel and a pick

And a walking stick

Hi ho, hi ho, hi ho..."

Soon three sacks are filled and I can't stop singing.

"Listen to young Freddie Steele" shouts Jack Winder, a well known union figure. "He's just discovered what real work is." Jack always forgets my real name and in consequence, usually refers to me as 'Young Freddie Steele'.

I'm too busy to look up but I hear a hidden voice from a nearby fox-hole, shout:

"That's rich coming from thee, Union Jack. Young Freddie's dug more coal in twenty minutes than tha's done in twenty years, and he's not pestering for a watter note" and everyone laughs out loud, including Union Jack.

When I clamber out of my fox-hole I notice there must be ten new miners following my dad's lead but the number in the whole field has mushroomed from a dozen to about fifty, including ten school kids. I look at my dad's face and it's 'black breet'* and I realise I probably look the same. Sweat is rolling down my face, so I take off my sweater and hat and sit on a sack of coal. I can actually see steam rising from my body like I've been on fire.

By now we have six hundredweight of coal in six sacks but there's trouble, literally, on the horizon. Parked on Broadway just beyond the Ambulance Station, is a police car. Two coppers are standing beside it watching us, but appearing to be content to keep their distance. It's like that scene in the film Zulu, when the enemy scouts are seen spying from afar.

"Right" says my dad "It'll not be long before police reinforcements arrive. Then they'll start moving us on, or worse. Six hundredweight will last me a good few weeks so I vote we do a runner. We can take the lot now or risk losing it all."

Then one miner starts to sing softly to the tune of *She'll be Coming Round the Mountain*:

"O I'd rather be a picket than a cop,

O I'd rather be a picket than a cop,

O I'd rather be a picket,

Rather be a picket

Rather be a picket than a cop"

And gradually the soloist is joined by the other miners and sack-fillers, then the small group develops into a mass choir and everyone's singing their hearts out. I love it. It's strange how singing like this raises your confidence and spirits.

"I've a better idea" I say to my dad, as the singing dies down a bit. "You look after the fox-hole while I wheel these sacks down to yours, and when I return, I'll bring Asa and he can hold the remaining empty sacks as you fill 'em?"

So, I set off before my dad can talk me out of it and soon there are three in our team from three generations – my dad, me and my eleven year old son, Asa. By now there are around seventy people on the spare ground and about 150 holes, in an area the size of a small football field.

Four 'Zulus' are now actually on the scene. I load my barrow with the remaining three full sacks.

"These coppers are actually alright" says my dad. "They've been talking to us. Three of them have family on strike. They've told us they're not going to bother us for an hour but then they'll be forced to make arrests if we don't move on. They say, if they don't take action they'll get it in the neck, themselves, from their Chief. So we have to get what we can as fast as we can."

I leave my dad and Asa to fill six more sacks while I disappear with my load. On the way down the cinder track there's a massive farmer's wagon with about a dozen young strikers sat on the back, making its way up to our new coal field.

Forty-five minutes later I'm back at our hole and we're done. We abandon our pit, feeling a great sense of accomplishment. Twelve hundredweight of coal will see my mam and dad through until the spring.

Following us down the track and away from the coal seam, are those enterprising young fellows, sat on the back of the wagon, carrying countless sacks full of contraband and singing:

"O I'd rather be a picket than a cop

O I'd rather be a picket than a cop..."

Heading the other way are two bobbies on horseback and two in a small police van with at least a couple of vicious Alsatians barking like hell in the back.

"Wouldn't fancy those wild bastards biting chunks out of me" I tell my dad as the van passes.

"I know" says my dad "and their *dogs* can be nasty bastards, an' all?"

I did enjoy my time as an honorary coal miner but my hands are in a mess, my back is breaking and my dodgy knee swells up like a football. Hence, the idea of trading my stick of chalk for a shovel is totally out of the question.

However, it doesn't stop me hobbling down to Leo's and buying some supplies for a fabulous family get-together at my mam and dad's house, that night; and I find celebrating, in the face of adversity, always generates much greater pleasure than in normal times.

Also, that evening, my dad tries out his newly-mined fuel and says he's never had coal of such high quality. Apparently, it burns slower and hotter than any coal he's ever come across.

* Local expression meaning, very dirty.

CHAPTER EIGHTEEN

OUT OF THE MOUTHS OF BABES - 1985

(Please note: Although this story is factually accurate, the names of places and people have been changed to avoid embarrassment.)

The 1980s is a time of school rationalisations as pupil numbers fall and there's a drive towards creating larger, cheaper-to-run, schools. Therefore, Barnsley Local Education Authority is undertaking studies to determine which schools should close and which should expand.

In Bridsworth, there are three schools, and the teachers at each one are anxious that theirs should remain open; so it's with some trepidation that our school, Kelly Road Primary, faces a courtesy visit from the town's mayor and his entourage, including councillors and Education Officers.

This news creates slight concerns for teachers but our head teacher cynically takes advantage of the situation by calling a staff meeting. Here, he emphasises the existential threat facing us and tells us that the survival of our school could depend on how impressed our civic visitors are. That means that attractive wall-displays, outstanding teacher performances and an impressive ethos could work in our favour. So with three weeks to go before the visit, the staff agrees to put on a bit of a show. Several places are identified as needing a facelift, after years of financial neglect. The paintwork inside the classroom and in the school hall is very shabby so we agree to cover the worst bits up with display paper and children's work. Recently, I've been given all the equipment needed to build an internal bird-hide and external bird-feeding table so this seems as good a time as any to get on with that. It's not a matter of pulling a rabbit out of the hat, it's more of a case of, let's make sure our visitors are fully aware of the great things our students are achieving.

I've dropped lucky this year. I happen to have a brilliant class of ten and eleven year olds. The vast majority are from the council estate, built to serve the local colliery, although to their credit, a few parents from the posh areas also choose our school for their children.

A lot of tough kids in my top-class (including the girls) are also sporty, creative and hardworking. That's a wonderful combination because in this particular area of our town, tough kids are regarded by their friends as leaders worth following. However, I do have one minor problem-child. His name is Darren and at ten years old he's a non reader. He has six brothers and sisters, some of which are now at the secondary school and all of them struggle with literacy. Every single one of the Lockwood children has a runny nose, no matter what time of year it is.

Darren is pleasant enough but he does lack something we all take for granted: He has no tact, or social graces, whatsoever. If he sees something unusual he'll make sure everyone notices it. For example, in the run-up to our mayoral visit, a School Inspector with a large purple birthmark on his cheek and forehead, also comes to our school on a friendly day-visit. As we are already well prepared for the mayor's visit this extra one doesn't really feel like an imposition. Besides, School Inspectors play a friendly, supportive role.

However, as soon as the Inspector appears in my classroom we run into problems.

"What's on that man's face?" asks Darren, as the poor Inspector enters the classroom. Darren's mate Paul puts his finger to his lips to hush him up but Darren's having none of it.

"Haven't you seen it, Paul? Urgh, it makes me feel sick" continues Darren, and as the Inspector goes bright red I have to intervene and apologise.

"Darren doesn't insult people intentionally" I say, softly, to the School Inspector. "He's a child with special needs and I try to make appropriate allowances. Please feel free to talk to my students and check out the quality of their work in their books and on display. This is quite a gifted class."

But Darren can't take his eyes off the Inspector with the pencil moustache and birthmark and even after the Inspector has finished his examination and makes his excuses to leave, Darren is still heard to say loudly: "I'm glad he's going. I don't like his face" and I give a pathetic chuckle and shrug of the shoulders as I close the classroom door when our HMI leaves. Darren is relieved but the look on the faces of the others, is something to behold. Michael has his eyes closed, Donna has her mouth wide open while she shakes her head, and Paul, Darren's best mate, has his hands up to his face with his eyes peeping through spread fingers. I open my mouth as if to speak but nothing comes out, then I open my mouth a second time but again I finish up saying nothing, and suddenly a huge spontaneous laugh bursts forth from everyone in the classroom except Darren. But Darren is looking round at everyone, as if to say, what's so funny?

It's no good punishing Darren or even explaining to him why his public comments are hurtful. I've tried it before and it's beyond his comprehension. Moreover, anyone who feels sorry for him is also a fool because I've discovered if Darren needs anything at all in life, he manages to get it by hook or by crook. Oh, he's a survivor, alright.

Thank goodness that on the day of the mayor's visit, Darren is off ill and although I'm reluctant to admit it, I confide in my colleagues that I'm secretly relieved. However, just before lunch, Darren does indeed turn up at school for his dinner and the afternoon session.

"I didn't realise you were on the 'afters' shift today, Darren?" I say.

"Er... I've just been helping t'dinner ladies put tables out in t'hall" he says.

"He told us he'd got your permission, Mr Steele" shouts Mrs Swift, the head dinner supervisor.

"No, Darren, you misunderstand" I say, talking directly to him. "I meant why haven't you been in school this morning?"

"There were no shoes left for me so I stayed at home, Mester Steele. I was going to come in my bare feet but I found these at t'bottom of our garden" he says, pointing down to the two odd wellingtons he's wearing.

"Oh I see. First up, best dressed, is it, hey?"

I take Darren to the staff room where I find an old pair of pumps in the lost property box that should fit him nicely. As he takes his wellies off I realise I've to find him a pair of old socks as well.

"It stinks in here, Mester Steele" says Darren turning his nose up.

I pretend to sniff under my armpits but the humour's lost on him. "It's only cigarette smoke from morning breaktime, Darren" I say, throwing stuff back into the lost property box. "Anyway, Paul tells me *you're* a regular smoker."

"Ey up! I don't smoke, Mester Steele" he says seriously.

"Oh, have you given it up, at last?" I say, teasing.

"No. I only tried it once and I was sick. Our John said my face went green. I'm not going to smoke, ever, Mester Steele. I don't like t'smell.

"Fair enough, Darren" I say. So are you ready to be on your best behaviour for the mayor this afternoon?"

What's the mayor, Mester Steele?

"He's just one of the councillors who runs this town" I say, as I send him for his dinner, and his parting shot to me as he walks through the school foyer is,

"Don't think I'll like that mayor bloke, Mester Steele, because I've heard my dad say, all t'councillors are bastards." I try to call him back but he's already disappeared into the hullabaloo of the school dining room.

Hmmm. That's all I need.

In the afternoon period we have Gymnastics followed by Creative Writing, then Design and Craft. As we begin our warm-up in the hall, the mayor, Councillor Roy Warden, his wife, Phoebe, and all their entourage make their way round all the classrooms. The design of this former secondary modern school building is such that the hall (which is also the gymnasium and dining room) has classrooms down three sides of it. Therefore, as our visitors move from class to class, they briefly enter our PE space and then disappear into another classroom.

When PE is over, my students are soon at work back in the classroom, re-editing or copying up their stories and poems and I have Paul on sentry duty near the half-glass door – just to warn us when it's our turn to expect our guests. I must admit I feel a little bit nervous as I think about how I'll cope if Darren's innocent but tactless insults, come to pass.

The mayor and his entourage all enter our classroom with friendly smiles on their faces. If only they avoid Darren and talk only to the other children, we'll be safe.

"Good afternoon children" says Mr Mayor.

Then the children chorus, "Good afternoon Mr Mayor. Good afternoon, everybody."

"You just carry on with your work and we'll come round and speak to you all if we can."

So far, so good. But of course of all the children they can speak to, who do they immediately make a bee-line for? Yep! Darren, the poorest looking kid in the room. The one who stands out a mile. Darren's finished his writing and moved on to designing and making a cat-mask using card, coloured crayons and knicker elastic. A group of about six adults are crowded around him and I can see they've entered into conversation but I can't quite hear their words. Darren could well be telling them to eff off because he's busy, and then where will I be? Oh dear! I feel like sticking my fingers in my ears and singing la la la.

After our visitors have talked to most of the children, spent time with our class pet mouse, Houdini, and observed new life in our snailery, the mayor approaches me to shake hands and says:

"A credit to you, Mr Steele. You've trained them well. When I asked young Darren if he enjoyed doing the work you set, he said,

"'I enjoy doing owt Mester Steele tells me to do'."

I smile graciously at what the mayor tells me but inside I'm thinking: Well done, Darren. That's my boy! I knew it. I knew I could rely on you. And just as I'm firmly shaking the mayor's hand I notice a blob of Darren's snot on the mayor's cloak and I just pray he doesn't notice it.

As a final act in my classroom, the mayor lets Darren try on his mayoral chain and bicorn hat. Darren can't believe it and doesn't stop talking about how incredibly heavy they both are.

Anyway, to cut a long story short, we are one of the lucky schools that are selected to stay open when school rationalisation is eventually implemented. Although, I do think it's very unlikely that decision was anything to do with our performance that particular day.

A second consequence of the mayoral visit was that from that time onwards I decide to deliberately draw attention to the disgraceful underfunding of State Education instead of foolishly covering it up.

Ian Bailey loves flying his model aeroplanes

CHAPTER NINETEEN

IAN BAILEY BUMPS INTO BRIAN GLOVER

"Of all the gin joints in all the world..."

It's Spring Bank 1990. The world is still celebrating the release of Nelson Mandela after 28 years imprisoned on Robben Island. Hundreds of thousands of people have been rioting in towns and cities the length and breadth of the country because of the hated new Poll Tax. Sinead O'Connor is top of the charts with one of the most beautiful ballads ever written: Nothing Compares to You. Meanwhile, in a popular Indian restaurant in Plymouth...

Ian Bailey is with a large group of friends. They've finished their meal and are enjoying a few beers after spending the day sub-aqua diving. Everyone's in a pleasant, relaxed mood. The noise levels are raised slightly because of the alcohol consumed, but you can still just about make-out the soothing, sub-continental, background music.

"Now there's an accent I recognise!" says a familiar voice from behind. Ian glances over his right shoulder and sees Brian Glover approaching. Ian is dumbfounded.

"Mr Glover! I can't believe it! Do you recognise me? I'm Ian Bailey. You taught me for a couple of years at Racecommon Road in the late '60s".

For a split second Brian is puzzled then it all comes flooding back.

"Recognise you? Of course I do. Ian Bailey, swimmer and scholar. Well, well, what an amazing coincidence," he says, holding out his hand for a sturdy handshake. "I recognised your accent a while back but I never twigged you were a former pupil. What a small world!"

Ian, still half taken aback, recovers some of his poise and decides to introduce all his friends, but by their open-jawed expressions he realises they all know who Brian Glover is, and so he simply says,

"Mr Glover, meet my friends," and there's a quick exchange of warm smiles and waves. "And please sit yourself down here," continues Ian, as he leans over and drags a spare chair into the space next to him, "and tell us how the world is treating you. This really is a most welcome surprise".

As he sits down Brian smiles and says, "It's Brian, by the way, not Mr Glover, and thank you. I'd really love to spend a few minutes having a catch-up".

They talk for a while about Ian's career since leaving school, about sub-aqua diving, piloting real aeroplanes and building and flying model planes. They go on to discuss Brian's successful career as an actor and writer and hear some of the many humorous yarns he's collected over the years. Brian is a wonderful raconteur and loves every minute of it but at the same time he makes sure no one in the group is left out of the conversation.

At one point Ian says, "And I bet you didn't know this: my older sister was a bridesmaid at your first wedding".

"What? No! Never! Really?

"Come on," says Brian, using this as the perfect excuse to celebrate further, "It's about time I got some drinks in. What are you all having?"

The first fifteen minutes of talk and banter soon turns into half an hour. The next time Ian looks at his wrist-watch he notices a whole hour has gone by, in the blink of an eye.

Finally Brian says, "I've so enjoyed your company but I'm sorry, I really must go now. Matinee performance at the Mayflower Theatre tomorrow".

Then he makes a special point of saying goodbye to everyone... and so ends one of the finest, most memorable hours of Ian Bailey's life.

Brian Glover: great actor, great teacher, great writer, great man! One of those very few people who, from humble beginnings, could truly walk with kings and still not lose the common touch!

"Of all the gin joints in all the world..."

CHAPTER TWENTY

MEETING BARRY HINES AGAIN AND SOME SIGNIFICANT SUBSEQUENT EVENTS - 1994

It's 1994 -almost 26 years since the closure of Longcar Central School. My car needs some repairs so I'm walking home from the bus station on this sunny, breezy, day, with a briefcase full of children's unmarked exercise books. Normally I would walk on Peel Street but for no reason in particular I decide to take a slightly longer route. I go up Pitt Street past the General Post Office and as I reach the Independent Book Shop under the YMCA I notice a big sign in the window. It says...

"MEET AND GREET AFTERNOON WITH KES AUTHOR

Barry Hines

Why not buy a book that Barry signs?

The Heart of it.

All welcome."

Wow!

At last, by sheer chance, I might be able to let the great man himself and know just how much all his former pupils appreciated him. I've waited 26 years for this opportunity.

The door to the Independent Bookshop is wide open, which makes it seem even more welcoming than usual. In the middle of the room is a large table where loads of elegantly arranged books are on display. Barry is talking to a middle-aged woman with a black perm and heavy make-up. When he asks for the 'dedication message' I notice his voice is just as I remember it. I see him unscrew the top off his beautiful fountain pen and make an inscription. I wonder if he'll recognise me after all these years. I don't think I've changed much but if I'm honest I'm three or four stones heavier and I look much nearer a 'slightly balding Bobby Charlton' than the skinny 1960s teenager.

"Can I help you?" asks the manager of the shop?

"Oh, thank you but no, I'd just like a word with Barry", I say, smiling politely and picking up one of the books on display. The fact is, as a bibliophile I adore looking round all bookshops but I don't want to be staring at shelves and lose my place as first in line to speak to Barry. And strangely, I wonder what I should call him. 'Sir', would be ridiculous, 'Mr Hines'? Far too formal, but would 'Barry' sound too familiar? No, 'Barry' will be just fine, I decide.

Then he turns to me and gives a warm, friendly smile. I can tell he doesn't know me.

"You don't recognise me, do you?" I say.

Barry takes half a step back and narrows his eyes like someone looking into a bright light. I see him stretch out his arm to hitch up his jacket sleeve.

"I'm Ronnie Steele," I say, grinning.

He takes a sharp breath like someone who's just had a shock, "Ronnie Steele!" he exclaims loudly. Then he says, "No. Sorry. Never heard of you", and a big, tormenting, smile spreads like the sunshine across his face. We both burst out laughing like teenagers, in front of the two new shoppers who've just entered the building. What a way to break the ice! Barry Hines hasn't changed one iota.

"Of course I remember you - Ronnie Steele, footballer," he says. "How are you? Come on, fill me in. What have you been up to since Longcar?"

I tell him briefly about all my football and educational ups and downs and he listens patiently with focus and courtesy, as if I was the most important person in the world. Then he says with conviction:

"I can't believe how similar your career path was to mine. "

What? This leaves me a little bit stunned. I've never once considered this. Have I been unconsciously walking in Barry Hines's footsteps all these years? Surely not. I'd have realised it, wouldn't I? I mention our former head teacher, Adolph Hopkins, and he shakes his head and says, "I based Mr Grice from Kes on Mr Hopkins, you know."

I tell him, "Great character but from a child's point of view I don't think you made Mr Grice, vile enough".

Then Barry talks about some of the very successful former Longcar students he taught, who've done really well in life and soon we get on to the topic of Brian Glover and have a belly-laugh over his larger-than-life antics.

Suddenly, in the midst of laughter, I look around and find that the small bookshop has filled up with Barry Hines' fans waiting patiently to get their own book-copy signed. We must have been in conversation for going on 10 minutes. Then Barry unscrews his fountain pen top and scratches a lovely inscription on the first page of my copy.

"I don't think you realise, Barry, just how much we all loved you at Longcar Central", I tell him as a parting comment.

He's not expecting this. He smiles and looks a bit embarrassed and says, "Aw, Ronnie, you must be taking the piss!"

And that's it. The last words he ever says to me... and they capture perfectly Barry's utter humility and lack of ego.

As I walk home I think of what Barry said about the similarity of our early careers and it dawns on me there are a couple of others that I'd forgotten. I'm a strong socialist and so is Barry and also I have faint ambitions of becoming a published author. However, I convince myself that had I never met this remarkable man I'd have still done what I did.

Seventeen years later, an article in the Barnsley Chronicle tells us that Barry Hines is suffering from severe Alzheimer's disease. I feel so, so angry with myself for not trying harder to visit him. I've been thinking about it for years but always dismissed it on the basis that Barry must be sick of being pestered because of his fame. Now it's too late. So I write a letter to the Chronicle mentioning Barry's great literary achievements but focussing mainly on him as a teacher. Moreover, I make one vital comment that was later to have a significant effect on my life: The people of

Barnsley, I write, must recognise the great achievements of Barry Hines by building a statue, in the town centre, in his honour.

The following year Barry's most famous work, Kestrel for a Knave, gets the ultimate recognition. Danny Boyle includes a clip from Kes in his marvellous opening ceremony for the Olympic Games. This spectacular show is designed to illustrate all the important aspects of British culture over hundreds of years and is broadcast to almost a billion people throughout the world. Out of hundreds of thousands of possible British achievements to showcase, Danny Boyle chooses Shakespeare, Brunel, The Beatles, The NHS, The suffragettes, the Royal Family and Billy Casper's kestrel flying from a wooden fence into his glove...

In the words of John Lennon: A working class hero is something to be!

Barry Hines with Casper

Photo courtesy of Margaret Hines

CHAPTER TWENTY-ONE

MY DAD IS MY HERO – Part Two

Mam and Dad are sat in the Smokers' Room on the Renal Ward at Sheffield Hallamshire Hospital. It's early January 1990 and the local lunchtime news is on the TV screen in front of them with the sound turned down. The low winter sun shines in through the closed windows and the cigarette smoke creates a fog that makes it hard to breath, even for people like my Dad who's been a smoker since he was fourteen. My Dad takes a look at the screen and he can't believe his eyes. There's a picture of a council flat, *their* council flat, the one they've only just moved into and it's surrounded by police marksmen.

"Did you see that, Mary? It was our new flat on Calendar News. I'm sure it was" he says, rising to his feet to turn the volume up, but by the time the TV is audible the programme's moved on to another story.

"Our flat?" my Mam chuckles as though Dad's hallucinating. "Why on earth would our new flat be on the TV news, Fred?"

"No idea but I'm absolutely certain, Mary. That was our flat. I'd bet my last penny on it" says Dad, preparing to push my Mam back to the ward in a wheelchair.

Dad catches the X32 bus back to Barnsley that evening and gets off on Babworth Road and walks it home along Hilltop Avenue towards Queenstone Village, on the edge of town. It's dark and there's no sign of any unusual activity around his flat so he phones me.

"Hiya Ron! It's only me. Your Mam's okay, so no need to worry, but I'm ringing you because today at the hospital the weirdest thing happened" he says.

"It's alright, Dad. I know what you're going to say" I reply. "You've heard about the gun siege at Joe Brashforth's flat. You know, that young blonde-haired bloke who lives in the same block as you but upstairs? They say he's threatened to shoot someone and armed police surrounded his flat until he gave himself up. My mate Karl says he's done 'time' before so you can bet your bottom dollar he'll have to do it again."

"Blood and sand!" says Dad, "I've lived near Queenstone for most of my sixty-two years and I've never heard of anything as bad as this. It's always been such a peaceful area. I hope this isn't a sign of things to come. I don't fancy living with your Mam in Dodge City."

"Oh, I'm sure it isn't, Dad. It's probably something and nothing" I say, trying to squeeze out a false laugh of reassurance.

However, it's soon clear that Joe Brashforth's presence in Queenstone is definitely an ugly blemish on the face of the neighbourhood. Nothing happens to him as a result of the police siege. It certainly doesn't herald a period of incarceration but it does signal the start of a terrible time for the elderly folk of the area, which is to last for more than a decade. Joe Brashforth is a massive brute with a team of obedient teenage disciples that he's recruited from the village. Everyone fears him, even those with a reputation for being able to "look after themselves" and the 'word on the street' is that he was forced out of Kexbrough where he once lived after creating utter mayhem there. Even the police avoid him because his vengeful victimisation knows no bounds. A detective who's married to a colleague tells me Brashforth once climbed into a farmer's field with a club hammer and bludgeoned a sheep to death. Then chopped it up and was arrested selling the meat in a local club.

Brashforth's reign of terror in Queenstone includes smashing the front windows of Mr and Mrs Elliot and three other retired couples. He's in his mid twenties but like Fagin he gets his young followers to do much of his dirty work. Irish Jack, for example, Second World War fighter-pilot hero, is tormented unmercifully just for being Irish. He has his car set on fire and mutilated rabbits thrown on his path. Brashforth's young hoodlums walk past his bungalow at the top of Raleigh Grove singing: "No surrender to the IRA". The fact that Irish Jack is actually a protestant means nothing to Brashforth. Eventually, Jack and his wife have to be re-housed by the council in a secret location. Furthermore, 90 year-old Mr Booker is so sick of the abuse, he shouts and waves his walking stick at Brashforth who snatches it away and breaks it in two. Later, a popular gay couple who live 50 metres away in the Square are so stressed by the constant baiting, they decide to sell up and live elsewhere.

We try to put our faith in the police to sort things but they seem to lack interest. They're forever being called out but are reluctant to take action even when there are witnesses. Perhaps they are waiting for someone to be killed first. Barnsley Council are not able to do anything as the flat Brashforth lives in is now privately owned and leased out. All the elderly victims begin to feel helpless and lose heart. "Roll on Boot Hill" one man in his eighties is frequently heard to say. They report incidents but never expect an arrest. After a while, Mr and Mrs Elliot's two grandsons' try a different strategy. They take matters into their own hands by knocking on Brashforth's door.

As he opens his door slightly he sees two young men with scarves hiding their identity. Each are holding what looks like a petrol bomb. Brashforth sees torn rags stuffed into the neck of each bottle and detects the distinctive smell of paraffin. Now things are really escalating to a very scary level.

"If you cause the slightest problems for Mr and Mrs Elliot ever again, these bottles are coming straight through your f**king window" whispers the tall one in the scotch plaid muffler. Got that?" Then both visitors walk off slowly and nothing more is said. Brashforth knows they mean business and thereafter, Mr and Mrs Elliot are left completely unmolested.

My Dad get his windows smashed, and the rail to his outside steps torn down. On another occasion Brashforth is seen throwing bottles at his flat. When it's reported, the police ask witnesses for photographs. I've never seen my Dad as frustrated. He's at his wits end.

Photographs? Photographs? Are you serious?" says Dad. "We've got witnesses who will testify. Isn't that enough? Do you want me to ask him to smile while I take a picture?"

"Now, now, Mr Steele. Calm down. No need for sarcasm." says one of the Police Officers, looking at his watch as though he has somewhere urgent to go. "We really don't want to have to arrest you now, do we?"

People around the village, gossip about why the police NEVER take action. One lunchtime, regulars in the Queenstone Social Club are overheard speculating that

Brashforth's a police informant and so he's untouchable, but again there's no definitive evidence for this and the atmosphere in the village deteriorates further.

Then comes a bit of good news: Brashforth is forced out of his flat and migrates 150 metres away to Longman Lane, just below the old church that's dominated Queenstone Hill for hundreds of years. Unfortunately, the harassment continues. Insulting graffiti is scrawled on Dad's fence. It's all misspelt but the offensive message is clear. Brashforth also falls out with an allotment-holder opposite his new rented place. One night the man's pigeon lofts catch fire and all 200 birds are burnt alive. No one really knows what's happened but everyone's thinks it's Brashforth who's responsible. The people of Queenstone stay silent because they don't want to be his next victim, therefore, the police make no headway with their investigations.

My Dad's living on the edge of his nerves. Around bonfire day he feels he has to keep a bowl of water behind the door, just under his letterbox, because he fears a lighted firework might be posted. He's not the only one living in terror.

At this time, Brashforth becomes more open about his fascist sympathies. At election time his windows and doors are festooned with far-right BNP posters and union jacks.

Then one summer's evening the beginnings of a solution is discovered. My Dad spends an hour down at Barnsley Cemetery putting flowers on my Mam's grave. He reads the inscription:

"In loving memory of a dear wife, MARY ANN STEELE

Died 18th February 1990

Aged 62 years"

My Dad starts to mumble:

I'm so, so glad that you died when you did Mary and didn't have to put up with this continuous harassment."

He feels an angina attack coming on and squirts his medication under his tongue. It brings immediate relief. Phew! He's lost weight as well and is now down to about eight stones. On top of that he's been recently diagnosed with prostate cancer. He's 74 now and we're not really expecting him to survive much longer. That same day, in the early evening I climb the concrete steps at the side of the Queenstone Road flats on my regular visit. The blonde-haired Brashforth is back outside the flats digging up some shrubs he left behind when he moved house. I watch him flip a spadeful of muck at Dad's windows and front door, which opens outwards and happens to be ajar. When Brashforth sees me, he and his young mate continue digging. I stand in Dad's doorway.

"Ey up Dad! Have you seen what this comic's up to?" I shout. Dad is quite deaf now and with the TV Evening News turned up he's not heard the machine-gun like sound of soil and small stones as they're thrashed against his bedroom windows and frosted-glass door. Dad emerges from his living room to see what's happening. "Look at the mess here. He's acting like a nutter again" I say.

My Dad is stood on the concrete path and I'm on the communal grass just a couple of metres away. Calling him a 'nutter' has provoked Brashforth's fury. Suddenly he bounds across to where I'm standing like a huge wild bull. His fifteen year old mate follows. I know this is it. It's fight or flee and I'm not going to run. I've not had a fight since I was a pupil at school and now as a forty-seven year-old school teacher I realise I'm probably going to get the hiding of my life and will almost certainly lose my job for brawling in the street. But things have gone beyond talking. Brashforth towers above me. With the sun behind him he's a silhouette but it doesn't lessen the filthy stink of tobacco on his breath. I'm waiting for his arms to twitch before I launch my punches which I fear will be like mere flea bites on his skin. Then suddenly I see him withdraw. He's falling backwards. In a flash, Dad has sneaked behind him, grabbed his throat with one hand and pulled him backwards to the floor with himself underneath. I'm now kneeling, punching Brashforth in the stomach as hard as I can while the Young Thug is grabbing my jumper and trying to pull me off. However, my punches make no impression. It's like punching the cushion of a settee. This is a fight to the death because I know if we don't win, me and my Dad are completely done for.

Then I notice something odd. The huge wild bull is not struggling quite as fiercely. Why is this? His strength seems to be ebbing and I know it's nothing to do with my pathetic punches. I stand up for a second to push Young Thug away but when I return to punch some more, Brashforth's arms are becoming limp. Dad is still on his back, on the grass, with Brashforth lying on top of him but I can clearly see Dad's fingers still tightly clutching Brashforth's throat. The monster drifts into unconsciousness. We are safe for the moment.

"Dad! Dad! Stop! You're going to kill him" I say. And Dad relaxes his grip slightly just to make sure the wild bull is not shamming. Dad then manages to roll the sixteen stone dead-weight off and stands up. Young Thug, me and Dad stare at Brashforth. He looks like the sleeping giant in my Daughter's old fairytale book. His lips and fingernails are purply-blue. My own right hand throbs with pain and when I look down, my first finger is all hideously mis-shapen. Brashforth is dead. I'm terrified. I can see the headlines in the Barnsley Chronicle:

"SCHOOL TEACHER AND HIS FATHER JAILED FOR MAN-SLAUGHTER".

But then I think I see the monster twitch and I'm almost certain his right arm moves. Then slowly, very slowly, he awakens and his lips and fingernails begin to return to their normal colour. After a minute or two Brashforth rises to his feet. He sways like a rotten old tree in the wind and then heads in the wrong direction across Queenstone Road towards Cherry Tree Inn, shouting: "Am gonna f**kin' fire thi for this."

Next day when I visit Dad he shows me a piece of paper. "This was posted through my letter box" he says. I study it. It's an artless drawing done in green biro showing a matchstick man throwing a flaming bottle through a window. My Dad and I both fear that 'fire' is Brashforth's modus operandi so we take the threat seriously. We both realise our nightmare is not yet over.

"Right! That's it! I'm going to put an end to this once and for all" I tell my Dad "and I'm not going to the police." As I leave his flat I'm already hatching a plan in my brain that I know will succeed. However, I can't get out of my mind how disastrous our lives would have become had my Dad continued squeezing Brashforth's throat for just a second or two more: from a well-respected family to prison lags in almost the blink of an eye. Henceforth, this experience makes me see the events of the world in a different light.

Isn't it strange how the fortunes of human beings are often determined by sheer, unadulterated luck?

Dad, four months before his death, on his last visit to see his friends in Skegness.

Dad recording

CHAPTER TWENTY-TWO

MY DAD IS MY HERO – The squeakiest wheel gets most oil.

The horrors of the last decade have led me to believe that for one reason or another the police have little interest in sorting out domestic or neighbourhood crime. Our experience suggests it's certainly not their top priority, anyway. With this in mind I decide not to report the Battle on the Lawn nor the serious threat of arson. My dad and I have to rid ourselves of this monstrous menace but without endangering our own freedom and reputations. Neither of us has even seen the inside of a courtroom never mind a prison cell.

I focus on the Elliot boys for inspiration. They managed to frighten Joe Brashforth off, so why can't we?

I phone up my nephews. I'd do anything for them and them for me. When I explain the situation, both are happy to be involved. Big Den is six foot six and built like a brick outhouse. His older brother, Mac, isn't quite as big but he's a thinker and as tough as Aberdeen granite. My son, Asa, and me make up a team of four. The plan at this stage is only to scare Brashforth so that Dad's no longer a target but at the same time not put my nephews, my son or myself in any danger.

So, we turn up at Brashforth's red-bricked semi on Longman Lane one evening about a week after he threatened to firebomb my dad's flat. None of us is carrying a weapon – this time. It's very hot and there's little wind. Speed and surprise are the key. We hear people talking and laughing in the back garden. I can smell cigarette smoke. I identify the unmistakable hoarse voice of Joe Brashforth and I feel nervous, but this HAS to be done unless we want to spend the rest of our lives in fear.

We burst in through the tall back gate like SAS raiders and immediately spread out about five metres apart down two sides of the square garden. Brashforth is in the far corner near an old hut with a new young lad next to him. I raise my hand like a traffic cop, as though to say, we come in peace. Brashforth grabs a spade and, holding it aloft, rushes towards me like one of those orang-utans in the jungle. But he stops about four metres away as I predicted he would. Everyone freezes.

"We've left our weapons at home this time" I say, as still as a cat.

"If you had brought weapons I'd have split you down the middle like a carrot" says the orang-utan.

"If we'd brought weapons you wouldn't be conscious now" says big Den as he stares at Brashforth like a hunter stalking prey. But Brashforth is clever. He somehow knows that the real threat comes from the quietest one in our group, so as he listens to Den's voice he keeps his eyes firmly fixed on Mac.

There's silence for a few seconds and I speak up again: "Take this as a genuine threat, Brashforth. Any more harassment of my dad and it'll not be a friendly warning. You'll not know when or where the attack is coming but be assured, it will definitely come."

And the whole thing is over quickly – in and out of the garden in less than two minutes having issued the solemn threat. Brashforth is aware now that my dad has at least four men willing to defend him. It's 2 – 0 to us but will he call our bluff and risk being violently ambushed at some unknown place and time? Based on the Elliot experience, I gamble he won't.

One week goes by, then two and nothing is seen or heard of Brashforth. Then one evening I'm walking my labrador on the spare ground where we once dug day-holes, foraging for fuel during the miners' strike. I suddenly bump into Brashforth and his young friends again. Oh no! I feel tense but I needn't.

"Oi! You can tell your father I'll not bother him again" he says, taking a huge draw on his cigarette and throwing the glowing stub onto the path. I say nothing but just nod and shout Max so I can attach the lead.

I feel incredibly relieved. I want to celebrate like I've scored some huge victory but I manage to keep po-faced, and head-off in the opposite direction with my dog by my side, looking up at me. I'm so happy that the harassment has finally ended.

At the age of 74 with heart disease and cancer you would have thought my father would have spent the twilight of his life relaxing and allowing others to assist him in his dotage. Nothing could be further from reality. Not only does he live another incredible fourteen years, he fills it with exciting adventures and on several occasions he appears to be almost indestructible. At times when his inevitable demise does seem on the cards he obstinately refuses to "go gently into that Good Night" but each time recovers, reinvigorated.

When he reaches 79 his health does seriously deteriorate once again though, and he's admitted into the Northern General Hospital in Sheffield. I get a call one Tuesday night asking us to come because he's not expected to last through the night. All six of his closest relatives gather in the waiting room waiting for the dreaded announcement. One of us bursts into tears and that sets us all off. By 5 am, dad refuses to depart this world quietly. A wonderful Egyptian consultant says he'll try to put a stent in dad's artery but he's not optimistic. Four hours later dad's sat up in bed in the Intensive Care Unit with a smile on his face eating scrambled egg and sausages. We can't believe it!

For the next six months my dad appreciates life more than ever. He's the type who likes to keep his house beautifully clean and tidy and loves singing on the karaoke at the Longcar Inn and the Shaw. He's often seen driving round Barnsley town centre on his invalid scooter displaying his novel licence plate "Fred One".

Unfortunately, by September his stent stops working effectively and he's admitted onto Ward 19 at Barnsley Hospital. We can't understand why he's put on this ward. Ward 18 is the Heart Ward not 19. After a week, Dad hasn't been seen once by a heart specialist nor has he undergone tests. He's in constant pain and when he presses the emergency button no one responds because they're all too busy. The ward is clearly under-staffed and all the elderly patients need intensive nursing. One old man, a retired GP from Wombwell, with Alzheimer's, keeps climbing out of bed and messing on the floor. Dealing with him takes up a lot of time that the poor overworked staff can ill afford. My grown-up son and daughter complain to me that my dad is being neglected though it's clear those on duty are doing their very best in impossible circumstances. I argue that this is the best place for him and the consultants surely know what they're doing. However, after two weeks and with his condition worsening, I give in to my children and phone up the hospital to make an appointment to speak to Mr Mohammad.

"Can I make an appointment to see Mr Mohammad, the consultant on Ward 19?" I say.

"I'm sorry, we don't have a Mr Mohammad at this hospital" says the receptionist.

"I've already met him a couple of times on Ward 19" I say, laughing "so I know he's definitely working there."

"Just a minute while I check again... No, sorry, you're wrong. We did have a Mr Mohammad but he left the hospital six months ago. If I were you I'd try phoning directly to the Ward. Thank you for calling."

So I phone Ward 19 direct and ask to speak to Mr Mohammad. "He's just doing his rounds now, Mr Steele" says a nurse. If you can get to the hospital in the next half hour you can speak directly to him."

I just reach the Ward as Mr Mohammad approaches my dad's bed. The pantomime continues. His assistant pulls the curtains round and out-steps Mr Mohammad to face me.

"Mr Steele, I'm very sorry to have to tell you this but I'm afraid your father is dying and there's nothing we are able to do" he tells me as he plays with a biro and pen top.

"Oh no he's not" I say. I suddenly realise my children were right and it makes me so angry. I trusted the doctors and nurses to keep me informed, to tell me the truth and try and give Dad the best treatment possible. I feel like smashing my fist against the emulsion-flaking hospital wall. Words pour out from me, slowly and perhaps menacingly:

"Tell you what, Mr Mohammad, if my dad's not in the Northern General Hospital by tomorrow morning there'll be hell to pay" and I leave Ward 19 believing that it is indeed nothing more than God's waiting room.

Next morning I get a phone call from the hospital telling me my dad's been transferred to the Northern General.

Squeakiest wheel gets most oil. How sad and wrong is that?

By Monday, Dad and I are having a very informal chat with one of the top heart consultants in the country. Peter Bradely, from Cawthorne, asks my dad how he spends his time. My father explains his love for televised sport and singing on the karaoke and how he's forever learning new songs. After a few minutes of animated talk, Mr Bradely interrupts him in full flow:

"Mr Steele, I'll be honest with you. The reason I asked that question was simply to find out how enthusiastic you were about life in general. You've convinced me that you're an inveterate optimist and would definitely benefit from a triple heart by-pass operation. Now don't get too excited yet because I have to persuade my colleagues to agree to this. You must bear in mind at 79 very few people are offered this expensive option" says Mr Bradely.

This is the biggest and best surprise of my dad's life. "Oh thank you! Thank you so much! Thank you God" he gasps, looking upwards as though he's in direct contact with heaven. "But hang on a minute. Why was I refused a by-pass when I was 69? What's the risks now and what's changed?" asks Dad.

"Medication was a safer bet when you were 69, Fred - May I call you Fred?" Dad nods, "But now your heart is in such a damaged state, surgery is your only option."

A few days later after many hours under the scalpal, my dad is recovering in Intensive Care after a quadruple, not triple, by-pass. One of his veins which they thought had 'died', was reparable after all. Dad does spend weeks recovering in hospital but except for a chesty cough, plus his long-standing prostate problem, his recuperation is uneventful. The five-star funding of the Northern General Hospital equates to five-star care for all their patients. But it still must be wrong to give extra funds to the big City hospitals by raiding the coffers of the local ones.

By the time he gets back home in Barnsley, my father's as fit as a 50 year old and he gets straight into making all his own meals and cleaning. Moreover, he begins spending money on smart, more youthful clothes and folk often comment on how fine he looks in his modern caps, smart leather jackets and trainers. On his return to the Longcar Inn he's cheered like a conquering hero. Some women form a group and nickname themselves the Fredettes. They stand on tables and chairs clapping, cheering and singing along, especially when he sings his *piece de resistance* song, *Human* by the Killers. He's even invented a robotic dance that turns his fans into a frenzy. Of course, Dad milks every minute of it.

My father and I also agree to go halves and buy a static caravan in Skegness. Consequently, he begins to spend every summer at the caravan, having a whale of a time singing with his new-found friends on the East Lincolnshire Coast. He's never still. I once turn up at the caravan with a bag of Salt's fish and chips and he's halfway through washing the roof and sides of the metal structure.

"Dad! We can pay someone to do that sort of thing" I tell him in admonishment.

"Nay, I needed something to do anyway" he says, squinting in order to identify stubborn streaks on the paintwork.

If I drive him into town for a walk round, we can't go ten metres without someone stopping him and hugging him and asking which pub he's performing in that night. Between the Clock Tower and The Lumley, Dad is the best known man in town.

He then goes through a worrying period of severe back pain which renders him housebound for a few months. The medical experts prescribe acupuncture and strong pain-killers but nothing works. We insist that he gets a referral to a consultant at the Northern General.

Squeakiest wheel gets most oil.

"I could try a lumber injection, Mr Steele, but it would be a waste of time and money" says the consultant looking at the x-rays. "You see, the nerves in the lower right-hand side of your back cause the pain you're feeling in your left leg. However, our scans and x-rays show the inflamed nerves are on the other side of your back."

I interrupt. "Please, do us one last favour: give my father one injection of the inflamed nerves and if it doesn't work, well... then it doesn't work and we'll just accept it." The consultant reluctantly agrees to this, just to shut us up, I think.

Squeakiest wheel...

However, the resulting injection works wonders - like a miracle in the bible. After one day, Dad is completely pain-free and at 85 he's performing on stage like a teenager. Nothing, it seems, can stop him but we both know he'll not last forever. Then just prior to his 87th birthday he's told that the prostrate cancer, which has been his silent companion for the last thirteen years is now residing in his bones; consequently, after thoughtful consideration, we agree to sell the caravan.

This time my father goes into rapid decline; so as a treat, I take him to Perry Dukes' studio to record him singing half a dozen of his best songs. Then me and my son also take him to a Skegness hotel for a couple of days in August 2015 so that he can see his old friends for the last time. They put on a huge party for him at the Boat House Inn and he shares out his discs so they have something to remember him by. When he returns home however, his energy plummets further and he becomes bedridden. I sleep at his flat in the armchair on some occasions but it's tough.

In November they accept him in the hospice for end-of-life care and we're told he'll probably not come out alive. His body starts to retain water resulting in his hands and legs ballooning up and discharging fluid. He's feeling depressed. I begin to wish he'd leave us peacefully in his sleep. He's looking very frail on his birthday on November 11th but he's delighted that the local vicar conducts a Remembrance Day Service in the hospice. He's never once, since World War II, missed going to the cenotaph ceremony outside the Town Hall.

Soon after his birthday the special love, care and top medical attention he receives from everyone at the hospice begins to improve his mood slightly and the swelling in his limbs does show signs of reducing. He begins to talk a little with his nurses, carers and visitors. A week later all the bandages are taken off, his legs and hands are normal and he's laughing and joking with all and sundry. It surely can't happen again can it? He's already made more come-backs than Frank Sinatra!

"Ron, I want you to pick me out a nice care-home" he says, looking round. "One that's like this place. By gum! I tell you what... it's wonderful here and I'm really enjoying my food now" he says polishing off his sweet. Unfortunately, I have to tell him that no care-home in the world can match the attention and medical facilities of the hospice, no matter how hard-working and well-meaning.

By the end of November, my dad's keys to the flat are handed in and all his furniture and personal belongings are shared amongst those who value them and he's as happy as a child at the fair. His new residence is the Galtee More Care-home. The place is recommended to me by a friend and everything is spot on: The workers, the food and the building are perfect but on that very first day, as I help him out of his wheelchair into an armchair, something catches my eye that causes me great concern: His left hand is slightly puffy.

Hey dad, your hand's swelling up again" I tell him.

"Oh don't worry about that, it's nothing" he says and changes the direction of the discussion. Every day after that, however, he gradually deteriorates and he becomes moody. He really needs the round-the-clock care that he had in the hospice but he's already had more than his fair share of that. The care-workers in the Home are so concerned they keep sending for his GP but his interventions are unsuccessful. I begin to think, if we can just replicate the treatment he got in the hospice... but it's too late. He becomes semi conscious and is taken to Barnsley Hospital A and E where me and his grandchildren gather around him. I ask him "What are we going to do without you?" and he whispers, "Just do your best" and not long afterwards he takes his final breath. He's pronounced dead on the evening of 20th December 2015... the date of my late mother's birthday.

His funeral is a magnificent affair with a full congregation, his favourite hymns, his own recording of Human, a beautiful coffin, plus spoken and poetic eulogies. To top it all, his nephew, Paul Wainwright, plays his favourite tune, Rodrigo's Concierto de Aranjuez, on the cornet in the echoing chamber of the church. Many of his friends from Skegness are also present. I feel both the happiest and the saddest I've felt in my entire life.

My Dad was only a slightly built man but fantastically strong, with the kindness of the Good Samaritan and the courage of a lion.

Now, whenever I hear the Killer's song I picture dad, doing his robotic dance and though I smile inside, my eyes inevitably fill up.

"Are we human

Or are we dancer?"

You don't have to be famous to be a hero!

My dad was my hero!

CHAPTER TWENTY-THREE

LOOK WHAT THEY'VE DONE TO MY SONG, MA – Murdering creativity

I hate teaching music because to be honest, I don't know the first thing about it. I can sing – although some might argue the toss about that - but I can't play an instrument and I don't know my crotchet from my elbow. So, for much of my teaching career I do what most primary teachers do, I 'cheat'. I record the Schools' Radio Broadcasts and practice the songs with the help of our extraordinarily talented school pianist, Catherine Newcome.

We're so lucky to have Catherine. When she works on school musicals with my colleague, Candy Gordon, the finished product is always something to celebrate.

Nevertheless, my personal ability to teach the subject never really improves and causes me much concern. Why can't I, or any teacher for that matter, inspire children to create a piece of music just like we do when we get them to create a painting, a model or a story? Why can't I create the conditions in school so that I can say to a pair of 10 year-old students: "You've an hour to compose and learn a piece of music of sixteen bars, to celebrate the Olympics or whatever? Anyway, that's my ultimate ambition, but the older I get the more I realise it's a pipe dream and that Music is a specialist subject requiring specialist skill.

That is, until I have an incidental conversation with Catherine:

"Be honest with me, Catherine, do you think it would be possible for a non music person like me to teach children to write music themselves?" I ask, as my class file into the specially adapted music room on bottom corridor.

"Yes of course, anyone can do it, Ronnie" she says matter-of-factly, as she gathers her sheet-music from under the piano seat.

What a revelation this is to me. For all these years I've wasted my time failing to teach music effectively and now I discover, it could well be possible. Hallelujah!

The following Monday, equipped with felt pens and white board, Catherine gets to work teaching my class about musical bars, beats to a bar and the value of a crotchet.

The children enjoy clapping out the different rhythms they've created. Even the students who find learning difficult, have no trouble following her instructions, including me. The half-hour just flies by. The following Monday, Catherine focuses on the value of the quaver, minim and semibreve which makes the task of clapping the rhythm a lot more challenging but achievable. Finally, in the third week she introduces 'musical pitch' using the glockenspiel – mainly because we've got enough for one between two for a class of 32. To keep it simple Catherine limits the children to using the pentatonic scale, which in layman's terms means five notes in sequence. Now we're all set to start creating our own music and it's taken only three half-hour lessons. Amazing!

During the next music lesson the whole class works collectively to create eight bars of original music, which is repeated so that, effectively, they're composing sixteen bars of music. Catherine then performs it on the piano and it sounds wonderful. The children are agog. Now they're desperately keen to compose and perform their own unique work of art. So they find a space to sit in the carpeted area and get to work, equipped with pencil, eraser, manuscript paper and glockenspiel.

There's lots of noise in the room and it's clear, all are fully immersed in the task. Among other things, they discuss the value of each note and its pitch. They discover that using semibreves makes playing easier but lots of quavers makes it more difficult. After about ten minutes the fastest working pair is taking it in turns to practice their masterpiece and soon the others catch-up and the music room becomes a cacophony of noise. It sounds like a room full of those tinkling jewellery boxes with the pirouetting ballet dancer, all playing at once. Ignorant OFSTED Inspectors would shake their heads and describe the scene as chaotic; shrewd educationalists would recognise that breakthrough-learning is not always incubated in monastic conditions.

By the end of the lesson the children are brimming with enthusiasm and want to show-off what they've achieved. When Catherine tells me no other class is using the glockenspiels at the moment I allow them to be taken back to my classroom so that the kids can hone their skills in their spare time. Furthermore, I know it's my turn soon to do an assembly so I tell them to prepare to entertain the whole school including the staff.

A fortnight later the children are confident enough to demonstrate their newly-found skills. The school hall is overflowing with children, teachers and expectation. The pupils' performances turn out to be stunning. They prove they are all capable of inventing, writing, reading and performing a piece of music and I realise for sure this is truly pioneering work. I'm so proud of what they and Catherine Newman have achieved, and can't wait to explore further possibilities, like:

Can we graduate to more complex, instruments?

Can our pupils create a piece of music to reflect a mood?

How do the professionals create a piece of music?

How did writers like the Beatles write their music?

Can we find out about the young lives of great composers in history?

What about creating a school orchestra that writes and performs its own music?

However, I soon appreciate we are facing some serious difficulties. Primary Education is not what it used to be. We, as teachers, are faced with a growing problem and it's this: Music, Art, Drama, Sport etc are increasingly being classed as low-status subjects because they don't feature in the SATs tests. As all state schools are forced to compete with each other in SATs or perish, schools are intimidated into narrowing the curriculum and focussing most of their time on the "core" subjects.

Furthermore it really is astonishing what's included in the SATs. If pupils know that "an adverbial clause is a dependent clause that modifies the main verb in the independent clause" the test scores of a school are raised, even though the finest adult writers in the world don't have a clue what the hell it means! In other words, in some ways, you might as well teach and test children on Latin, for all the good SATs does. The truth is, the broad curriculum is being cut down and perverted and the schools are becoming little more than exam factories. Every drop of pleasure is being squeezed out of the process for teachers and learners with few real benefits. Fear reigns supreme.

At our school, we're frequently invited into the head teacher's office to discuss results and targets, as SATs scores become the new mania. The pressure to focus on these things to the exclusion of everything else, gradually becomes overwhelming. Kate Banks, Joanna Young and I, who train two school football teams, have to reluctantly abandon them because our workload is far too onerous. We detest having to do this because we know how important sport was to us at school.

So after much introspection I have to accept that my enthusiasm for creating Music comes at the wrong time in history. 35 years ago it would have been embraced with enthusiasm but in the 21st century our new, young head teacher believes it's necessary to gear everything towards improving SATs results.

Then comes the bombshell. Catherine Newcome is told her services will no longer be required by the school. It's not made clear exactly why but for whatever reason I'm gutted for her and angry. She's in tears. Some of the staff have worked with her for more than twenty years.

Over the coming few months and years the old guard is forced out, one by one, and more pliable teachers and assistants are employed in their place. But the children's test scores are counterintuitive. Instead of improving, they stay roughly the same. Moreover, the school's inspection reports are also deteriorating. It reminds me of those Victorian explorers in Australia who run out of food and eat the non nourishing vegetation they find in the bush, only to become even weaker and eventually die. I suppose the old adage "If you're in a hole, stop digging" is being completely ignored and there's no alternative strategy to fall back on.

The changes the new head makes eventually reaches the point where OFSTED judges the school to be failing and it publicly announces that the school's in Special Measures.

The head teacher is sacked.

In the words of the ballad:

"Look what they've done to my song Ma...

They've picked it like a chicken bone and I think I'm half insane, Ma."

Fortunately for Catherine, some schools recognise the educational value of music as well as the pleasure it can bring, and so she continues to be successfully employed at other primary schools in the Barnsley area.

Catherine Newcombe, a musical genius.

CHAPTER TWENTY-FOUR

BARRY HINES' FUNERAL - MARCH 2016

On 20th March 2016, Barry's friend and poet, Ian McMillan, announces his death to the world. I've been expecting it for ages and I tell Janet, my partner, if it's a public funeral, I must go to show my respects and, if possible, make everyone aware just how brilliant a teacher Barry was. Some might not know this, and they should. I pour my heart and soul into a poem, dedicated to Barry and contact the vicar, Reverend Hale, seeking permission to read it at the Service. Reverend Hale promises to ask Barry's widow for her permission but he doesn't get back to me by the day of the funeral, so we set off to St Peter's Church at Pilley with my eulogy neatly folded in my jacket pocket.

During the Service there are some wonderful tributes paid to Barry -from his children and from Ken Loach, Richard Hines, Ian McMillan and Producer Tony Garnett. Then Reverend Hale asks the congregation if anyone else would like to speak.

This is my big chance.

I raise my hand immediately and get called to the lectern. I take out my papers and unfold them and feel confident. I start speaking with a nice, slow, clear delivery and the smiles and laughter of the congregation tells me that what I'm saying is chiming with them. The only slightly uncomfortable thing is, Reverend Hale is hovering nearby and I fear he's about to cut me off before I've read it all. But I'm wrong, and as I end the poem there's a spontaneous cheering and applause. I'm quite stunned and pleased by this and I think, wow, this is surely the first time this ancient place of Christian worship has witnessed such celebrations.

Here are the final two verses of my poetic eulogy:

"But more down to earth is what he'd like

So I'll tirelessly campaign

To get Barry Hines The Special One

A statue in his name

Some went to school to obey the law

Some went to avoid the mines

Some went for the love of learning

But I went for Barry Hines"

After the ceremony the family go to the graveside to bid their last farewells. Barnsley Chronicle reporter, Mike Cotton, stays just outside the church, eager to interview me. He's particularly interested in the concept of building a statue in Barry's honour, and promises to help all he can. I feel so delighted that people have heard about this and that at least Mike Cotton is taking me seriously.

Jean, Barry's second partner, is very gracious. She invites Janet and me to the wake and tells us just how much she appreciates the poem.

"I lived with Barry for years but had no idea how popular he was as a teacher until I heard you today. Thank you, Ronnie, it means a lot", She says, still red-eyed from mourning. She tells me about a lecture she witnessed Barry delivering to PE teachers in Wrexham in which Barry was given a very hard time, so she is particularly pleased with my testimony.

"Reverend Hale behaved a bit oddly", I say, as I still try to make sense of his anxious behaviour.

"Yes", she agrees, looking puzzled. "He looked like he was about to stop you. But you needn't have worried. We were mesmerised by your contribution and just wouldn't have allowed him to."

Some of the mourners ask for a copy of the poem to be sent by email. Then we enter into a conversation with film producer, Tony Garnett, who relates a hilarious story about Brian Glover and the Longcar head teacher, Mr Hopkins and then it's time for us to depart.

I have this intense feeling of satisfaction. I achieved what I set out to: all those at the funeral are now aware that Barry was a truly inspirational teacher. Now I have a statue to build.

When I arrive home I open my emails and I'm surprised to find one sent earlier that morning from Reverend Hale saying Barry's widow doesn't want me to read my eulogy. Oh dear. No wonder he was very uncomfortable. I reply to him apologising and explaining my error was a genuine accident. He never replies. I don't think he believes me.

CHAPTER TWENTY-FIVE

THE TOPSY-TURVY WORLD OF STATUE-BUILDING

Our journey on the road to success is full of ups and downs, which I suspect is always the case in projects of this nature. However, the exhilarating successes far outweigh the disappointments. In 2011, in a letter to my local paper, I first raise the idea of building a outdoor statue in Barnsley town centre, in honour of Barry. At his funeral, five years later, I propose this again. Now all the big-talk is over and it's time to consider practical ways of getting one made and paying for it. This is new territory for me but the challenge of exploring the unknown has always thrilled me. However, on more than one occasion during the next three years, I begin to doubt that it can be achieved at all.

Mike Cotton, the Barnsley Chronicle reporter, writes a fairly regular piece for me, asking for volunteers to join a statue-building committee. He puts me in touch with one of the best sculptors in the country, Graham Ibbeson, who happens to live only a couple of miles away. I always had Graham in mind because with his talent, experience and the convenience of him living nearby, he's the obvious choice. He's a huge fan of Barry's work and tells me, as a former secondary modern student himself, he has always identified with Billy Casper, the hero of the film, *Kes*. Graham was thinking about retirement but considers this project too great a temptation; it will be a labour of love for him, where, by fierce negotiations and waiving certain fees, he can reduce the overall costs to a minimum. He comes to me one day in 2016, full of enthusiasm, with a file of his plans. They are very detailed and comprehensive with sketches and costings. Janet Richardson, my partner, is also keen to get involved. Janet taught in the English Department at Hoyland Kirk Balk Comp, years after Barry taught at the school. During the 1990s she named the school junior library, The Barry Hines Library. Next to volunteer is the bestselling author, Milly Johnson, who also lives quite close. Then a Labour Councillor from the Barnsley St Helen's Ward also offers to help. Wow! This is going to be easier than I first thought... but I soon realise, nothing could be further from the truth. The problem is, we're finding it impossible to recruit anyone suitably qualified to fill the role of treasurer. Weeks, then months go by and despite regular appeals in the Chronicle and social media, no potential treasurer comes forward and without a treasurer we can't start to raise funds. I'm also told that to achieve success it's vital we get Barnsley Council on board. So I speak with them and they appoint a Council Officer to liaise between our group and the Council. He has lots of recent experience in this field and his first pieces of advice are extremely useful. He tells us we must expect no financial help from the Council and that, as a legal requirement, we must create a constitution. I contact an old friend, Steve Wyatt, from the Oaks Statue Group, who sends me their made-to-measure constitution. Tweaking it for our purposes is not difficult but it's time-consuming. It takes many weeks of adding, amending and deleting until it's finally agreed by the committee and then passed fit-for-purpose by officialdom. We are proud to include in it, a paragraph promising that any money leftover will be donated to Barnsley Independent Alzheimer's And Dementia Support organisation (BIADS). This feels particularly poignant since Barry Hines himself was a sufferer. The liaison officer is also very keen for us to create a "Time-line, plan-of-action" but until we get someone to look after our finances, this is futile.

The committee meets monthly at my home but we're having problems. A couple of meetings are arranged but illnesses and other emergency commitments lead to last minute cancellations because we can't reach a quorum; this and the fact we don't have a treasurer, leads to a general feeling of frustration.

Although she'd prefer not to, Milly offers to take on the role of temporary treasurer until a permanent one can be found. However, very soon afterwards... bingo! Jan Brears steps forward with the perfect credentials. I arrange an interview in the temporary Public Library on Wellington Street and I feel she's exactly the person we're looking for. She's had a long professional career in finance at the Town Hall and has worked as treasurer on other successful projects. I welcome her on board, subject to good references. The references I receive from professionals I know, are terrific. Our group is then further strengthened when local film-maker, Carl Yeates and a photographer, Kris Branigan, join us over the Xmas period, 2017. It's now late December, 2017, over eighteen months after Barry's death, and at last, everything's in place and we can begin to raise funds. I'm feeling incredibly relieved!

Sadly, by the end of January 2018 our group appears to implode. Janet and I are on holiday abroad but still in communication by email with everyone associated with the Kes Group. Now that all the tough spadework has been completed, one of the committee members decides to launch a coup d'etat. He sends an open letter to the group saying that the whole project is being badly organised and suggests some things must change. As I've been the only organiser up to now it's very clear who he's campaigning to replace. At the same time the liaison officer is livid about a TV interview Milly and I did just a few days before my holiday departure, in which we suggest a particular town centre site for our statue. He also claims the project has stalled and he's so concerned that we haven't yet created a time-line of aims, he orders the Kes Group to suspend the project immediately and indefinitely. He warns that unless we agree to this, the council will withdraw its support. It's a classic Catch 22 situation: End the project and the Council will support us; refuse to end it and we'll be abandoned. Meanwhile, the coup-plotter resigns when he gets no positive support from the rest of the group. Then the Labour Councillor also sends in a letter of resignation in solidarity with the Officer. The absolute truth is, we're now in a terrible pickle. Out of eight people attending meetings, three of the most powerful and influential have gone. I'm close to despair. I know Janet will work to the bitter end for success but what about my other colleagues? Have they also started to lose faith? I'll never totally give up on my quest but I really don't fancy starting from scratch again with just me and Janet.

Then comes a pivotal moment: I receive an email from Milly Johnson. I'm expecting the worst. Another resignation will probably sink us. However, when I open it I get such a wonderful surprise. She says that the recent activity has hardened her determination to make a success of our project. We will not fail! We'll show them, alright!

What an effect this has. Everyone in the group feels lifted and re-energised. It's just the shot-in-arm we need. Yes, we'll succeed even in the face of adversity. Then Graham announces defiantly that he's going to start the sculpture of Billy Casper and his kestrel even though we don't have a penny in our account. This really is a leap of faith and further reinforces team morale. It's now that I first realise the absolute necessity of having a team of people who are not just capable, but more importantly, can work well together. The doomsayers might not realise it but their actions have spurred the rest of us on.

By the summer, 2018 we're catapulted into the 21st century when Stuart Gibbins, a friend of Milly, kindly creates a website for us free of charge and our film-maker and computer expert, Carl Yeates, creates a Facebook page and email address.

Then we enter another period of minor disappointment. We've set our target at £106,000 and the general feeling is, we should be able to raise about £40,000, through one of the crowd funding sites, within weeks. All the feel-good stories emanating from such internet sites suggest that making thousands of pounds in a very short time is a cinch. Our actual results, though, tell a different story. When our period of raising money is up, we've only accrued the relatively small sum of two grand and we've have to pay eight per cent of that to the organisers. Two thousand pounds will certainly not impress the council, that we're now trying to get back on board. We arrange a meeting with Councillor Roy Miller at the Town Hall. If we enter the meeting with such a paltry amount accumulated, it will not augur well. Therefore, three of us in the Group decide to each order and pay for a statuette at £5,000. Now we can go into the meeting with a Kes Group bank balance of a healthy looking £17,000 plus.

Our meeting with Councillor Miller and senior Council Officer, Sue Theideman, goes very well. The liaison officer who said he would withdraw Council support is not present. Councillor Miller and Sue Theideman are welcoming, gracious and give us a fair hearing but it's worrying how little they know about our decisions thus far. Councillor Miller asks if it's true that Barry Hines hated Barnsley? He's also concerned that our statue is one of Billy Casper displaying the iconic two-fingered salute. We're all astonished. We've spent a year establishing reasonable aims, fully expecting the liaison officer to pass this information on to Councillor Miller but it appears there's been a major breakdown in communication. So we explain that Barry's depiction of Barnsley people, in his work, is testament to the love he had for our town. As for the statue pose, we show the Councillor and Sue Theideman, photocopies of Graham's decidedly uncontroversial design (I decide it's not wise to inform the pair that twelve months earlier I did argue for the two-fingered salute but was out-voted). The outcome of the meeting is brilliant. After a fair exchange of ideas we are given the Local Authority's blessing to carry on.

In July 2018 the world starts to take our project much more seriously when we hold an Open Day to view Graham's clay sculpture before it's sent off for casting. It's such a lovely summer's day outside Graham's studio and everyone's in a celebratory mood. It's very well attended by the media, by Mayor Steve Green and Council Officers. Labour councillors, Linda Burgess, Roy Miller, Pauline Markham and Wayne Johnson demonstrate vital support and encouragement. We know for sure that nothing's going to stop us now.

It's on this day that we meet an extraordinary man. Phil Crowe, originally from Barnsley, is working in Los Angeles for a company that does special effects for the Hollywood film industry. He's a great admirer of Barry Hines and offers to help the group. Phil goes into overdrive flogging our statuettes, home and abroad and before we know it, he's made about £20,000 worth of sales.

From here on, we have no more group meetings because we find they're unnecessary. Instead we throw ourselves into fund-raising activities and communicate with each other by email or face-to-face at real events. My trade union and political experience comes in handy because it's made me reasonably confident in addressing an audience. So we get ourselves invited to scores of meetings in order to elicit financial support. The brilliant Barnsley artists, Barry Thornton and Richard Kitson donate paintings for auction. Many local trade unions and businesses give very generously. Lots of top-class local musicians volunteer to entertain and raise cash. We also make two grand out of the Tesco Bags of Help Scheme. I manage to sell a few of my poems and part or all of the money goes into the fund. I even get some of my framed pictures from home that I'm bored with and auction them off. Milly's friend, the writer, Willy Russell, appears at the Penistone Arts Group and donates over a thousand pounds to our cause. We sell at more local galas and festivals than I ever knew existed. It's very hard work but little by little we are starting to build up a tidy sum. Errors of judgement are made, like the early concert we organised at Carlton Club which only profits us by about £300, but we learn from our mistakes and do far better next time. Local celebrity, Dave Cherry and Alan Jones, plus our own Carl Yeates, all organise lucrative music fund-raisers.

During this period we also identify a second misconception. The group invests £4,000 on merchandise in order to advertise our project and inflate our bank balance. This should go a long way towards reaching our target. We're selling t-shirts, tea-towels, hessian bags, mugs etc. However, it eventually dawns on us that if we sell every single item at double the production cost, we're still only going to make a total profit of £4,000. That's a heck of a lot short of the £106,000 needed in total. But the positive thing is, this merchandise gives us a reason to be present at most galas and festivals in and around the local area and leads to sales of the real money-making products: the statuettes.

It's these statuettes that are turning our ambitions into reality. They are exact copies, but scaled-down versions of the life-size clay statue, originally created by Graham. The actual scaling-down is done through photo-scanning technology and Graham pulls off a masterstroke by persuading the scanning firm to generously waive the £2,000 fee. All these statuettes are limited editions. The sixty resin ones at £150 each, soon sell out. Those made out of solid bronze at £5,000 also sell out pretty quickly and we find our medium-sized bronze ones at £1,500 each, are equally popular. In the end about 60 to 70% of our funds come from the sale of these wonderful creations.

During the summer of 2018 I get invited to speak to a group at the Holiday Inn in Barnsley. As I get down from the stage a woman approaches me. It's Anne Scargill from the Women-Against-Pit-Closures, fame.

"Excuse me" she says "but are you in contact with Richard Hines, Barry's brother, by any chance? Richard taught my daughter, Margaret, and she'd love the opportunity of getting in contact with him to thank him for being such a wonderfully supportive teacher when she was at junior school."

I tell her I'm not yet in contact with Richard but as soon as I am I'll ensure some kind of communication is arranged, if possible.

A few weeks later I do manage to contact Richard and we spend several weeks exchanging emails. He's delighted with our project and also very pleased to be put in contact with Dr Margaret Scargill. Richard also arranges to take our group on a tour of the sites in Hoyland where *Kes* was filmed. Furthermore, he sends us ten signed copies of his brilliant book, *No Way but Gentlenesse*, to help increase our funds. His tour of the various film locations is just magical.

During this period the finished, life-size, bronze statue arrives from the foundry, packed like a precious dinosaur egg in the back of a van. It's temporarily displayed in the Experience Barnsley Museum at the Town Hall. The whole operation goes like clockwork with much interest from the media. We're getting good at this.

Over the next twelve months cash keeps flowing in. By learning from our earlier mistakes we manage to have a spectacular concert in March 2019 at Dodworth, Station Road Social Club. Fred Fletcher, who played Judd in *Kes*, tells me his two sons play in a band and would be happy to perform free of charge for a fund-raiser. That evening the band, Mayhem, performs brilliantly, cleverly tailoring their songs to the needs of the packed, mixed-age, audience. Fred buys loads of *Kes* videos off the internet at a reduced price and sits at a table most of the evening, autographing and selling them. In addition he slips a hundred pounds from his own pocket into our cash box. I display my £5,000 bronze statuette to let the punters know that although they've all been sold, there are still a few £1,500 smaller ones available. I'm approached by Barry Hayes, a big *Kes* fan and a popular Manchester businessman.

"How much did you say this little beauty costs?" says Barry, keeping his eyes focussed on it.

"Five grand."

"Tell you what I'll do" says Barry, "I'll give you six grand for it."

"Sorry Barry, it's not for sale."

He tries again. "Okay then what about seven grand?" he says, fully expecting me to give in.

"You don't understand, Barry, the answer is still no. Even if you offered me a hundred grand, I still wouldn't sell because it means more to me than money" and as I speak I fully expect Barry to phone for a psychiatrist to have me sectioned. "You see, Barry, this statuette is a symbol of my youth, and of Barry Hines and of all the work we, as a group, have put into our project. It feels like part of my very soul." By now Barry Hayes has given up hope but I do let him know that I'll make enquiries as to whether Graham is willing to sell the Artist's Copy. A few days later I contact Barry Hayes to tell him the Artist's Copy is indeed available if he still wants it and he snaps it up immediately.

That evening at the Dodworth Club, taking into account the sale of, CDs, two statuettes, merchandise, many donations and an auction, the Kes Group makes a whopping profit of approximately £6,000! It just shows what a difference experience makes. What's changed is that now we're NOT charging an entrance fee and we don't bother messing about putting a buffet on. These are simple changes but effective.

During the spring of 2019 we're faced with another huge obstacle which threatens to derail our ambitions. We lobby the council for a busy, outdoor, town-centre site for our finished statue. We feel it would be very fitting to get it installed in or near the brand new public library that is about to open. Time after time we make a good case but each time it's rejected. Instead we are offered two backwater sites where it'll hardly be seen by the public and could be subject to vandalism. Janet and I go into town and do several pedestrian surveys to measure foot-traffic and prove the offered sites are relative wastelands. Thank goodness Sue Theideman takes cognisance of the graphs that Kris Branigan produces from our raw data.

Eventually, we are given an opportunity to investigate possible, acceptable sites with various Town Planning Officers and fifteen are identified. This is whittled down to three which we would be pleased with, so we, as a group, vote on our order of preference. We're all so excited. All we need now is for the Council Cabinet to pass it and they've never been known to veto recommendations like this before. It now seems all cut and dried; time to celebrate, we think. So imagine our dismay when we're told that all three acceptable sites are refused and instead we're offered a place INSIDE the new library. I'm full of frustration, especially when a couple from the Labour Party in Hoyland tell me that one senior Labour politician makes it known that he'd prefer the statue to be "buried on a corner in Hoyland because no one in the area liked Barry Hines, anyway". I rail against the indoor site. Our statue was conceived, designed and built of materials suited for outdoors so that it could be appreciated by the maximum number of people. We might as well have spent £25,000 on a fibreglass statue rather than many times more on a durable one. Moreover, what are visitors from other towns or even countries going to do if they turn up in Barnsley and the library is shut? I also fear that once it's installed in the library it'll never see the light of day again. What a waste! However, the rest of the group feel confident that when the town improvements have been completed an outdoor site will be found and so I'm outvoted. The statue is heading for inside the library. I consider resignation but Graham and Janet patiently persuade me that my fears are unjustified and that when the dust settles we will indeed get our outdoor site.

A few weeks later, during June 2019, our concentration is focussed on another huge event. Milly Johnson feels it's important to do something in Hoyland to show our appreciation for giving us the remarkable Barry Hines. Therefore, she's keen that our group pays for a Blue Plaque through the Yorkshire Society. This turns out to be another stroke of genius, giving us more kudos from the people of Hoyland. That hot July day turns out to be our finest so far. A large crowd turns up and we are delighted that Kes director, Ken Loach and producer, Tony Garnett, travel north for the day. The local media and lots of helpful and supportive councillors are also out in force. Barry's good friend and author Ian Clayton is also there. A wonderful brass band leads the march to the house where Barry lived when he wrote *Kes*. Barry's brother, Richard, performs the unveiling and after a couple of speeches and photographs we return to the Saville Square Pub for a generous reception subsidised by the landlord. Del Scott Miller performs his beautiful ballad about Barry Hines then The Barnsdale Hood Duo continue with their lovely brand of folk music. Another good thing to come out of the day is that Dr Scargill and her former teacher, Richard Hines, meet face to face for the first time in over forty years.

"Bet you were thrilled to meet up again after all these years" I say to Richard, as I set up the speaker system inside the pub.

"Thrilled? I'd not recognise her if I met her, Ronnie. She was a ten year old child the last time I saw her. I think she's probably changed a lot since then." So I bring Margaret and her husband, Jim Logan, over to re-introduce them. As I return to my technical chore I hear them all talking away animatedly. That evening the local TV and radio news is dominated by our successful ceremony. It leaves us all with a very satisfying after-glow. I find sharing a team success is always more enjoyable than an individual one.

The only tiny error we make is that we could have invited ALL those at the Blue Plaque unveiling, to Saville Square for food. More than half of the high-quality buffet is left to waste. We'll not make that mistake again. When we have the big unveiling of the statute in the centre of town, everyone's going to be invited to the buffet.

All our lobbying and activities are suspended in 2020 because of COVID-19 but in March---- 2021 we are at last offered an outdoor position in the town centre. Graham and Janet were correct after all. It's not the site we lobbied for but nevertheless it's superb: just outside the entrance to the modern Alhambra shopping Centre, right in the heart of the main precinct.

The official unveiling is planned for October or November 2021. The whole group awaits the day with tremendous anticipation.

During the spring of 2021 we agree to loan our replica, fibreglass statue to Hoyland library. As part of his legacy we also plan a Barry Hines Annual Writing Competition for children and adults with kestrel trophies for the winners. Moreover, we believe that the residue in our bank account when everything is paid for, and which is destined for BIADS, will be substantial.

A Kes Trail, using fibreglass kestrels, is also planned in order to link up all the statues in the town centre.

If someone asks, has it all been worth it? I'll say, of course it has and I'd do it again ten times over for the remarkable, Melvin Barry Hines.

Now I can die happy.

But I'll not complain if I get another twenty years of terrestrial fun...

Richard Hines, Barry's brother unveils Barry's Blue Plaque at 78 Hoyland Road

Sculpture design by sculptor Graham Ibbeson

Barry's Grave

BUILD IT AND THEY WILL COME

And come they do, in their droves, from every corner of Yorkshire and beyond, to see our statue for the very first time. The unveiling day, in his own town, organised by his own people, is a celebration of the wonderful work of Barry Hines.

Ken Loach, Dai Bradley, Ian Clayton, and Sally Hines (Barry's daughter) all speak glowingly about Barry and in praise of his well-deserved statue, created by sculptor Graham Ibbeson.

As the brass band plays *When the Saints go Marching in,* the late autumn sun makes an appearance and the people who turn up on this momentous day, gasp in awe as the blue veil is delicately slid off. It's a sight that so many people have waited so long to witness and to cheer.

Everybody's eager to congratulate the Kes Group for making all this possible without ANY financial help from the Council but we all respond in the same way: This is not our day, this is Barry Hines's day.

The positioning is our second-choice site - we initially hoped the sculpture would be accommodated in the new town square. Nevertheless, it's still a prime spot where people from all areas of town will be able to come and admire it on a regular basis.

Finally, as one of our main sponsors, Phil Crowe, said recently:

"Your successful project shows what wonders can be achieved when ordinary, determined people come together."

Phil is absolutely right but I also want to add that our small, happy band of Barry Hines' admirers would never have succeeded without the help of the trade union movement, the business community and the thousands of individuals throughout the world who have backed our campaign.

Barry Hines was a true working class hero and in the words of John Lennon, "A working class hero is something to be".

"If Barry Hines had not written books
And fame had passed him by
I'd still worship this school teacher
Paint his name across the sky

But more down to earth is what he'd like
So I'll tirelessly campaign
To get Barry Hines, The Special One
A statue in his name

Some went to school to obey the law
Some went to avoid the mines
Some went for the love of Learning
But I went for Barry Hines"

Part of Ronnie's eulogy, spoken by him at the funeral of Barry Hines, in April 2016.

Barry Hines (1939 – 2016)

Photo courtesy of Margaret Hines

A few examples of the hundreds of tributes paid to Ronnie about his writing:

"Fabulous, fabulous, fabulous. Can't wait for the next [story]!!! Great writing; grips the reader's attention and leaves them wanting more!!!"

Kathy Britton

"A gripping storyline and so true to life... Brilliant read and brilliant story!"

Rita Stone

"I don't know what you do for a living, Ronnie but whatever it is, your talents are wasted. Can't wait for next week's chapter. Write the book!"

Anne Lawrie

"Hi Ronnie. Thank you for sharing this with me. I can honestly say I have never been so moved by a historical piece as the one I have just been reading. If you have not done so, in my view, your writings should be published."

John Jackson

"Holding my breath. Can't wait for Part Two."

Moll Brown